365
COCKTAILS

DUNCAN BAIRD PUBLISHERS

LONDON

365 COCKTAILS

MIXERS • SHAKERS • SHOTS

THE COMPLETE BARTENDER'S GUIDE

BRIAN LUCAS

PHOTOGRAPHY: WILLIAM LINGWOOD

365
COCKTAILS
MIXERS • SHAKERS • SHOTS
THE COMPLETE BARTENDER'S GUIDE

Brian Lucas

First published in the United Kingdom and Ireland
in 2003 by
Duncan Baird Publishers Ltd
Sixth Floor
Castle House
75–76 Wells Street
London W1T 3QH

Conceived, created and designed by
Duncan Baird Publishers

British Library Cataloguing-in-Publication Data:
A CIP record for this book is available from the
British Library

ISBN: 1-84483-084-5

Typeset in Eurostile
Colour reproduction by Scanhouse, Malaysia
Printed in Singapore by Imago

Editorial Consultant: Rebecca Miles
Managing Editor: Judy Barratt
Editor: Zoë Stone
Managing Designer: Manisha Patel
Studio photography: William Lingwood
Stylists: Joss Herd (cocktails), Helen Trent

10 9 8 7 6 5 4 3 2 1

Publisher's Note: The alcohol rating used in this
book is intended as an approximate indication of
the alcoholic content of each cocktail and should
not be relied upon for any legal purposes, such
as the driving limit. The cocktails in this book
are intended for the consumption of adults, in
moderation. Neither the publishers nor the author
can accept responsibility for any consequences
arising from the use of this book or from the
information contained therein.

contents

introduction

The first bar I ever set up was a student bar in Cape Town called Lloyds – a success only because of the thousands of students who lived within the two-mile radius and came in for the famously cheap drinks. But it gave me a taste for what it is like to be the reason that people are having a great time. When I arrived in London in 1993, I used the bar trade to make cash to fund my travels. This turned out to be my best decision ever – I ended up working in bars all over the world, slowly increasing my knowledge of drink-making. Finally, in 2000, I set up my first official bar in London – the Goodge Bar, a small, oddly designed cocktail bar and restaurant, where I trained up my protégés Tim Stones, Ryan Tyler and Duncan Sawichi – to name a few. I've never looked back.

They say that the bartender never forgets the first cocktail he or she ever mixes. For me it was a Vodka Martini (see cocktail no.9). I mixed the drink with one part vodka and two parts vermouth, and I was so proud! You live and learn – later that night I was informed that the martini should have been made with two parts vodka and that the vermouth is used only to line the glass. I was crucified – but it taught me that making cocktails is a fine art and one that I hope to pass on to you in the pages of this book.

For me, mixing drinks is about taste. I take my time to produce a drink to perfection and I revel in the pleasure of invention. I love to watch the faces of people as they drink my cocktails – sometimes they look content, sometimes they look surprised, but they always seem to ask for another! Why don't you sample my favourite creation – the Grape Escape (see cocktail no.246). The drink has a cool balance of grape and brandy (try it with two sprigs of mint as a summer cooler). And if it is me who is drinking? Whiskey is my tipple and my favourite cocktail is the Old-fashioned (see cocktail no.211).

My greatest wish for this book is that I can give you some of my sense of fun and adventure in making cocktails. The 365 cocktails have been chosen from my database of more than 4,000 to include sophisticated classics, modern twists on the old classics, and innovative new mixes. I hope that, once you have mastered the basics of mixing drinks, you will want to experiment and extend your cocktail repertoire well beyond the scope of anything that I can teach you. Everybody is different, and we all prefer our drinks in a certain way. All the cocktails can be altered to suit your individual style. Don't be afraid to add or subtract ingredients, to substitute a mixer with fresh fruit, or to swap the listed liqueur for your personal favourite. And, if you are ever in London, you might find me in the Salt Whiskey Bar or the Fly Bars – drop by and tell me about your own new creations, I'd love to hear about them.

I wish you fun and happiness in mixing these drinks – enjoy!

Brian Lucas

cocktail basics

Where does the word "cocktail" come from? What was the first cocktail and who were its first drinkers? What have been its changing fortunes? Since the dawn of time, the human race has found ways of intoxicating itself – sometimes for ritual or medicinal purposes, often for enjoyment. Drink has been at the heart of such merrymaking for thousands of years. In some respects, the cocktail represents a coming together of drinking fads and fashions from all time. From the Romans, through US Prohibition, to the present-day glitterati, cocktail-drinkers span not just decades but whole eras of history.

In this chapter we start by looking at the changing fortunes of the cocktail from its earliest beginnings to the present day. Then, we take a look at some of the practicalities of mixing cocktails at home: what drinks and mixers will you need to stock a bar? What garnishes should you have to hand? What cocktail-making equipment and what glasses will you need? This chapter presents the answers to these questions along with a host of other practical bartending tips and explanations to help you make all the cocktails in this book to absolute perfection.

The Story of the Cocktail

If the definition of a cocktail is a blend of two or more different drinks, then who can say when the first cocktail was mixed? Was it in ancient Egypt or ancient Rome when alcohols and spices were mixed into medicinal elixirs? Or in Aztec Mexico, where sacrificial ceremonies were performed in a haze of intoxicating spirits? We have to look forward to the 14th century to find what might be the first documented blended drink – the "bragget", a mix of mead and ale. In fact, the Middle Ages have a lot to answer for in the history of cocktails. Many of the key ingredients in the cocktails we drink today (especially many of the liqueurs) have medieval origins: apothecaries and monks used wines and spirits to preserve medicinal herbs, or to infuse the health-giving properties of herbs to make medicinal tinctures, and over time (often several hundred years) these developed into commercially produced drinks. However, it wasn't until the 18th century that anything resembling a modern cocktail came into being. While Europe can lay claim to developing the sophisticated distillation and production techniques for all the major spirits used in cocktails, it is the United States that must take pride in the creation and export of the cocktail phenomenon itself.

The word cocktail first appears in a US dictionary in 1803. Here it is defined as "a mixed drink of a spirit, bitters and sugar". However, debate rages over the word's origin. Some say that in the wild days of riverboat gambling on the mighty Mississippi, big winners were invited to wear a red cock's feather in their caps and to mix a drink using every spirit behind the bar. This would be drunk in a glass shaped like a cockerel and stirred with a spoon resembling its tail. Others claim that, in the days following the American Revolution, a feisty innkeeper by the name of Betsy Flanagan served meals of roast chicken to American and French soldiers. The birds for the roast were stolen from a pro-British neighbour and not a bit of them went to waste. After supper, Betsy entertained her guests with drinks at the bar – she decorated each drink with a tail feather from the unlucky fowls. "Vive le cock tail!" called the French.

However, perhaps the two most plausible of the many stories about the word cocktail are also rather less colourful. French Creole Antoine Péychaud opened his apothecary in old New Orleans in the 1790s. To measure out the spirits for his medicines, he used an eggcup – a *coquetier* in French. Alternatively, and probably most likely of all, our word cocktail is derived from the French word *coquetel*, the name given to a certain mix of wines (the actual recipe is lost to history). It is possible that Major General Lafayette, a French nobleman who helped fight against the British during the American Revolution, brought the word with him to America when he arrived in Philadelphia in July 1777.

In whatever way "cocktail" came to be in that American dictionary, with new refrigeration techniques, the commercial sale of ice and waves of immigrants all bringing their own ideas, 19th-century America saw the birth of several cocktail drinks we now regard as true classics – the Sazerac (claimed by many to be America's first cocktail; see no.217) and the Mint Julep (see no.194) to name but two. The early 1900s were a time of great experimentation, and the hotel bars of the rich and famous (the Waldorf-Astoria being one) became cocktail playgrounds with new creations emerging almost daily. The craze for cocktail bars quickly spread to Europe and in 1911

Harry's New York Bar was opened in Paris by US bartender Harry MacElhone (Harry's Bar was later to become the birthplace of such classics as the Bloody Mary). Even Prohibition, which hit the US in 1920, could not quench the thirst for cocktails – in fact, it ended the exclusivity of cocktail-drinking and brought it to the masses. Prohibition outlawed the production and sale of all alcohol in the US and its laws were not fully repealed until 1933. During this time alcohol consumption went "underground" into illicit bars, known as the "speakeasies". Here, the bartenders had to be creative in order to mask the flavour of poor, bootleg liquour. As a result, different drinks were mixed together and served up as new and intriguing concoctions in themselves (fruit juices became common ingredients in cocktails to hide the taste of rough alcohol). Meanwhile, in Europe, a continent recovering from the rigours of World War I, people leapt at the sense of freedom and glamour given by sipping delicious drinks in fancy glasses. The cocktail golden age of the 20s, 30s and 40s was born.

If this was the golden age of cocktails then it was also a time when some of the most famous people in the world made us realize just how fashionable it was to be photographed with a cocktail in hand. Cocktails and cocktail places began popping up in literature and film. The Daiquiri is first mentioned in F. Scott Fitzgerald's 1920 novel *This Side of Paradise*; the Dry Martini is famously supped by Dean Martin in a host of Rat Pack entertainment (movies and cabaret alike). Famous faces were linked with famous bars throughout Europe and the Americas. Ernest Hemingway is perhaps the era's most prolific, celebrity cocktail-drinker. A regular at Harry's Bar in both Paris and Venice (he recounts scenes in the Venice bar in his novel *Across the River and Into the Trees*, written in 1950), the Bloody Mary is said to have been invented especially to cure his hangovers. When in Cuba, he was a frequent visitor to El Floridita in Havana, where he sat at the bar to watch his cocktails being made (he is also said to have invented the Papa Doble there – a double Daiquiri) and brought many of his famous friends, among them Hollywood movie stars Spencer Tracey and Errol Flynn, to join him in sampling his favourite mixes.

Despite Hemingway's most valiant efforts, after World War II there was a general dip in cocktail consumption throughout the world, but especially in Europe (some say that 1950s America was a period of "atomic" cocktails – drinking buoyed up by post-war optimism). By the 1960s, in Europe and the US, when free love and more altered-state forms of intoxication were popular, the meagre cocktail was nowhere to be seen. It wasn't until the 1980s that things looked up again for cocktails. With fresh ad campaigns for brands such as Martini and Cinzano, and the launch of new brands such as (more recently) Absolut, came renewed interest in mixing drinks. Now we can enjoy cocktails in cocktail bars old and new in every town and city in the world. Try the Rainbow Room in New York (at sunset on a clear day is best); watch the rich and famous go by at the Sanderson in London; imagine yourself sat next to Ernest Hemingway himself at Harry's Bar in Venice (arrive by gondola – it's the best way – and if you are there during the Venice Film Festival, expect to rub shoulders with A-list movie stars of the time). No matter what its changing fortunes in the past, the cocktail is a feel-good drink and always has been. With spirits and liqueurs getting ever more sophisticated, we might think that the story of the cocktail has really only just begun.

How to Use This Book

The purpose of this book is to give you an array of cocktails with which to experiment and enjoy. Some have been chosen because they are classics in the cocktail world. The most important of these classics are given special feature pages in the relevant chapter of the book. Each of them is labelled to identify whether it is a traditional (created earlier than 1960) or modern classic and each is given a short history so that you can find out why it deserves its classic status. However, there are many other cocktails in the general listings that you will have heard of – including such famous blends as the Singapore Sling and the Cosmopolitan, so be sure to flick through the whole collection. All of the cocktails have been selected (from my personal database of more than 4,000 cocktails) to give you a range of ideas to both delight and challenge your palate, as well as enthrall your guests. Each recipe serves one person, unless otherwise specified.

The book is divided up into chapters according to "base" ingredient – the ingredient in the cocktail that will most influence the flavour. All the major spirits have their own chapter (vodka, gin, tequila, rum, the whiskies and brandy), as well as champagne. Chapter eight lists cocktails using "liqueurs and other spirits" – alcoholic drinks that make some of the most interesting cocktails available, but which don't warrant a chapter on their own (for example, the almond-flavoured liqueur amaretto and the apéritif Campari, as well as a host of fruit liqueurs). Non-alcoholic cocktails conclude the book and feature some delicious and interesting fruit blends for the drivers and teetotallers at your party.

All of the 365 cocktails are numbered (cross-references between cocktails refer to the cocktail numbers, not page numbers). Every cocktail has a little table. The first line in the table indicates the kind of glass that the cocktail should be served in (see pp.22–3 for a key to the symbols). The second line shows an alcohol rating in a series of filled or part-filled circles (◐○◑●), representing one-quarter, one half, three-quarters and one whole. One filled circle is roughly equivalent to one unit of alcohol. However, the alcohol ratings have been adjusted to allow for certain effects that mixing and preparing the cocktails might have on the alcoholic nature of the drink. For example, a vigorously shaken cocktail marginally loses some of its alcoholic content; while cocktails with several different spirits (especially if they are different colours) can have a more alcoholic effect on the body than their "unit" quantities might suggest. Similarly, the unit system does not account for the amount of alcohol by volume (abv; see opposite) in certain spirits – adjustments have been made for very alcoholic drinks, too. The alcohol rating is intended only as a guide to alcoholic content and should not be relied upon for any legal purposes, such as the driving limit or the limit for operating heavy machinery. Beneath this is a star-rating system (showing a minimum of one star to a maximum of five stars), which is my personal take on each cocktail. If I think you should definitely try a cocktail, I give it a star rating of 5; if, however, I think a cocktail is one only for days when you are planning to experiment, I give it a rating of 1.

Finally, at the end of the book are a series of "reference lists". These lists organize the cocktails according to mood or occasion – so, for example, if it's not gin you are looking for, but something to cool you down on a hot summer's evening, turn to these lists to find the top 10 "Summer Cocktails".

How to Stock a Bar

In a well-stocked home bar it is essential to have the basic spirits and fine liqueurs, as well as a range of mixers and a variety of suitable garnishes. In addition to the basics, there is a rich cornucopia of other spirits and liqueurs which you may like to collect over time as you experiment with a wider selection of cocktail recipes and develop your own preferences. The following pages form a guide to the main spirits, mixers and garnishes that appear in the cocktails in this book – the more of these you can amass, the more fun you can have! Explanations are given for more unusual drinks.

SPIRITS AND LIQUEURS

Having bottles of good-quality scotch, Canadian, Irish and rye whisk(e)y, as well as bourbon, vodka, gin, tequila, rum and brandy in your bar will cover the basic spirits you need for the majority of the cocktails in this book. To find out more about each, read the introduction to the relevant chapter, where I explain the origins and the distillation techniques for the base spirits. Other spirits, such as fruit brandies, are listed below. These sometimes form the cocktail base, but more often than not are used as delicious flavourings. Liqueurs are highly sweetened, spirit-based drinks flavoured (by a variety of techniques) with one or more (and sometimes more than a hundred) herbs, spices, fruits, flowers, barks or seeds. The following list is a glossary of some of the weird and wonderful spirits and liqueurs you might find in the perfect bar. Each entry gives a rounded "alcohol by volume" (abv) percentage. Just as you might expect, abv gives an indication of the alcoholic strength of each drop of drink. A note to the uninitiated: the mixture of generic and brand names used in the world of cocktails can be confusing. Where possible, I have stuck with generic names unless a particular brand really is what's needed for a certain cocktail. Also, under the definitions of some generic names, I have mentioned some of the common brands you may come across for ease of reference. Finally, some unique liqueurs that have been around for hundreds of years are known only by their brand names – this, too, will be indicated in the definitions.

Absinthe: *see* **Pernod**

Amaretto: An almond-flavoured liqueur, commercially produced in Italy since the late 18th century (but perhaps invented in 1525). It is made by macerating (soaking) almonds and apricot kernels (principally) in neutral spirit. (30% abv)

Anisette: A sweet liqueur made by macerating 16 different seeds and plants and blending the maceration with a neutral spirit and sugar syrup. Anisette should not be confused with Pernod (see below), which is made using star anise (the fruit of the evergreen, Chinese star anise tree) rather than aniseed (the seed of the Mediterranean anise plant, a member of the parsley family). (25% abv)

Bénédictine: Created in 1510, making it perhaps the world's oldest liqueur, Bénédictine is the brand name of a sweet, herbal liqueur first made by Bénédictine monks in a Normandy abbey. The recipe, which has never been successfully copied, includes 27 plants and herbs. The drink takes three years to produce. (40% abv)

Bitters: A generic term, sometimes given in its Italian form *amari*, for a range of bitter-tasting alcoholic drinks made from macerating a mix of bitter flowers, roots, fruits and peels in a neutral spirit. Bitters are most commonly used in small quantities to give a cocktail a distinctive, non-sweet flavour. The well-known brand Angostura bitters (invented in Venezuela in 1824 but now produced in Jamaica; 45% abv) and orange bitters (20% abv) are the two types of bitters most frequently used in cocktails.

Campari: A bright red *amaro* (bitter), Campari was invented in the 1860s by the Milanese café-owner Gaspare Campari. This extremely dry liqueur (usually drunk as an apéritif) has a strong quinine flavour. (25% abv)

Chambord: A brand name for a distinctive, French black raspberry liqueur. (25% abv)

Chartreuse: Chartreuse, a brand liqueur, has been made by Carthusian monks in southeast France since 1603 (but the recipe itself is believed to date from much earlier than this). At any one time only three monks are permitted to know the secret recipe, which contains 130 different herbs and spices. Two different varieties are available: green (invented by the monks in 1745) and yellow (1840), of which green Chartreuse has the higher alcoholic content (55% abv compared with 40%).

Coconut Liqueur: A sweet-tasting liqueur made by steeping fresh coconut in light rum. (20% abv)

Cream Liqueurs and "Crème de" Liqueurs: There is a distinct difference between what we call "cream liqueurs" and those known as "crème de". A cream liqueur is a heavy, sweet cream-based liqueur with a relatively low alcohol content owing to the high proportion of cream. The only cream liqueur used in this book is an Irish cream liqueur of which Bailey's Irish Cream (17% abv) is by far the best-known brand. This has a whiskey base.

"Crème de" liqueurs (20–30% abv) are rich, sweet liqueurs that are dominated by one particular flavour but do not contain cream. They are usually made by adding fruit concentrates to a base spirit, and occasionally by adding essential oils. Their names are sometimes anglicized, hence you may see "crème de banane" called simply "banana liqueur". The following types of "crème de" liqueurs can be found in my recipes: crème de cacao (cocoa and vanilla); crème de cassis (blackcurrant); crème de framboises (raspberry); crème de menthe (peppermint); and crème de mûre (blackberry). Crème de cacao can be found in both brown and white varieties and crème de menthe can be either white or green. In each case the flavour is the same – the selection of one over the other is usually to do with the esthetics of the cocktail.

There are several other liqueurs dominated by a single flavour which are known more commonly by an anglicized version of their names (or, alternatively, by a brand name) rather than a "crème de" name. These are listed separately.

Curaçao: An orange-flavoured liqueur made by soaking the bitter peel of the curaçao orange (from the Caribbean island of the same name) and several other ingredients in a mixture of water and neutral alcohol and then re-distilling to release the fruit's essential oils. The distilled fruit is then blended with a neutral spirit or brandy. Curaçao can be coloured for visual effect, the most popular varieties being orange and blue. (20–40% abv) *See also* **Triple Sec**

Fortified Wines: Madeira, port and sherry, made in Madeira, Portugal and Spain respectively, are all ordinary wines fortified with another form of alcohol. In the case of Madeira (20% abv), this alcohol is something called "deaf wine" – a grape juice prevented from fermenting by the addition of brandy. Port (20% abv) is fortified simply by adding a neutral spirit during the fermentation of the grapes. Doing so prevents the grapes from completing fermentation, resulting in port's sweetness. Sherry (15–20% abv) is fortified using a neutral spirit once fermentation is complete. A basic rule for including these drinks in cocktails is to buy an expensive brand as it will definitely make for a better drink. *See also* **Vermouth**

Frangelico: Named after the 17th-century Italian monk who created it, this is a sweet, hazelnut liqueur made by steeping hazelnuts, berries and a host of other secret ingredients in a neutral spirit. (25% abv)

Fruit Brandies: Strictly, a fruit brandy is a spirit that has been distilled directly from the fruit iself, usually from the flesh and, where relevant, stones. However, cocktail-makers these days use the term "fruit brandy" also to mean a fruit liqueur (see below). As a general rule apple brandies are readily available in the strictest sense. Other fruit brandies are probably easiest to find labelled as "fruit brandy liqueur".

True apple brandy is distilled directly from apples. Calvados (after the region in France where it is produced; 40–45% abv) is probably the best-known. However, calvados now has an equally good, younger US cousin, known as applejack. To avoid any confusion, the recipes in this book always list "applejack or calvados" when true apple brandy is required. "Apple brandy" refers to apple brandy liqueurs. True cherry brandy is known as "kirsch" (or Kirschwasser in German; 45% abv). As with apple brandy, the recipes list kirsch when the true brandy is required. Reference to "cherry brandy" means that you can use cherry brandy liqueur. Apricot brandy means the brandy liqueur; simply because it is easier to buy than the brandy distilled from the fruit.

Fruit Liqueurs: Any alcoholic drink in which the fruit has been infused in a base spirit. Strawberry liqueur is one of the most popular and is used in several of the recipes in this book. *See also* **Fruit Brandies** and **Schnapps**

Galliano: An Italian brand liqueur first made in Tuscany by distiller Arturo Vaccari (he named it after a famous Italian general). Galliano is golden in colour and is a ssweet blend of more than 40 herbs and fruits, all overlaid with vanilla. (40% abv)

Kalúha: A Mexican brand of coffee-crème liqueur. Tia Maria offers a good alternative. (25–30% abv)

Madeira: *see* **Fortified Wines**

Maraschino: This clear, Italian cherry liqueur is made by macerating (steeping in a neutral spirit) the whole marasca cherry (stem, skin, flesh and stone). Marasca cherries that have been preserved in this way take the name "maraschino cherries" – often used as cocktail garnishes (see p.17). For the maraschino liqueur required in these cocktails, invest in a jar of maraschino cherries and use the preserve. (30% abv)

Midori: A Japanese brand of sweet, bright green melon liqueur. (20% abv)

Parfait Amour: The generic name for an unusual, highly perfumed liqueur. Parfait amour is based on crème de violette with a citrus orange twist. (25% abv)

Pernod: A liquorice-tasting spirit, which gained popularity in the early 20th century as a substitute for the widely banned absinthe (see Absinthe Special; no.326). Pernod replaced absinthe's wormwood (which is a hallucinogen in large doses) with star anise. (45% abv) *See also* **Anisette**

Pimm's: *see* Pimm's Cup; no.277

Port: *see* **Fortified Wines**

Schnapps: Original schnapps is a high-quality grain or potato spirit (similar to vodka) originating from Scandinavia (*schnapps* is actually a nickname meaning "gulp!" – the drink's proper name is aquavit or *akvavit*), which is then re-distilled with its flavouring (most commonly caraway seeds). Today, the term schnapps is more often used for fruit-flavoured liqueurs. The most common is peach schnapps. Peach, peppermint, apple and cinnamon all appear in the recipes in this book. (45% abv)

Sherry: *see* **Fortified Wines**

Sloe Gin: A red-brown liqueur made by steeping sloe berries in gin. (25–30% abv)

Southern Comfort: Created in New Orleans in the 1860s, and first commercially produced in St Louis, this popular branded drink is an American whiskey-based liqueur flavoured with more than 100 ingredients, but principally peach. (40% abv)

Strawberry Liqueur: *see* **Fruit Liqueurs**

Triple Sec: Considered a type of clear curaçao (see above), triple sec (40% abv) is made by macerating the peel of sweet and bitter oranges in neutral spirit. The most famous brand of triple sec is Cointreau. Grand Marnier (made by macerating bitter oranges in cognac and adding sugar syrup; 40% abv) is often used as a triple sec. Although this is not strictly accurate (there are no sweet oranges in Grand Marnier and it is not clear but golden in colour because of the cognac), the distinction is rarely made in cocktail-making, and it has not been made in this book.

Vermouth: A basic, dry white wine, infused with herbs and then sweetened and fortified. The name vermouth itself comes from *Wermut*, the German word for wormwood, and the drink is developed from the medieval practice of preserving medicinal herbs by steeping them in wine. A well-stocked bar should have a bottle each of dry and sweet vermouth. Dry vermouth is pale golden in colour (and usually comes from France) and sweet vermouth has been sweetened with sugar and coloured with caramel. Several well-known brands of vermouth are available, of which Martini, Cinzano and Noilly Prat are perhaps the most famous. (15–20% abv)

MIXERS

A selection of non-alcoholic ingredients are also required to keep a well-stocked bar. Some can be bought and others should ideally be freshly made as and when needed.

Carbonated Drinks: Soda water, lemonade, cola and ginger ale are essential.

Coconut Milk: A milky liquid from the second pressing of fresh coconut (popular in Thai cooking). This should not be confused with the sweet and sticky coconut cream.

Cream: Both single and double cream are used in the cocktails in this book.

Egg White: This is always listed as optional. If you choose to include egg white in your recipe, be aware that salmonella can be contracted by eating infected, raw egg (the bacteria are killed off during cooking). Note that raw egg should never be given to children, the elderly or pregnant women.

Fruit Juices: Where possible, for best results use freshly squeezed juice. You will need orange, lemon, lime, cranberry, pineapple, grapefruit, passion fruit and tomato juices.

Fruit Purées: These are commercially available, but you can create your own fruit purées by chopping and blending the fruit with some sugar in a kitchen blender (if you make in bulk, purée can be frozen). The main purées you will need are strawberry and raspberry.

Sour Mix: A blend of lemon and lime juice and sugar used as a cocktail flavouring. The mix can be bought, but I prefer to make my own. Combine 14 ml (½ oz) of lemon juice and 14 ml (½ oz) of lime juice with a dash of sugar syrup (see below).

Sugar: Make sure you have a good stock of powdered (caster) sugar. Brown and white granulated sugar is also required for some of the recipes.

Sugar Syrup: Sometimes called "simple syrup" or "gomme", sugar syrup is used as a sweetener. You can buy sugar syrup, but it's easy to make yourself. Combine equal parts sugar and water in a pan and bring to the boil. Simmer and stir, adding more sugar until the mix is viscous. Cool and store in an airtight jar in the refrigerator.

Syrups and Cordials: Sugar syrup, grenadine (a pomegranate-flavoured syrup), lychee syrup (taken from a tin of lychees), orgeat syrup (almond-flavoured), raspberry syrup, papaya syrup, passion-fruit syrup and lime cordial are all essential.

Vanilla Extract: A flavour made from vanilla beans. Make sure you use "pure" or "natural" (not artificial) vanilla extract.

GARNISHES

Fashions come and go but there are a few basic garnishes you will need (remember that garnishes are often used to flavour a drink as well as to decorate it). In addition to those listed below, keep to hand some fresh mint, nutmeg, cocoa powder, cinnamon and crushed nuts — and some straws and swizzle sticks, too.

Celery Sticks: Preferably left with their leaves on, celery sticks are placed in a drink (usually bitter or refreshing drinks) and can be used by the drinker like a stirrer.

Cinnamon Sticks: These delicate and fragrant sticks are placed inside the glass.

Citrus Fruits: Orange, lemon and lime can be cut variously to provide a range of garnishing effects. A *wedge* is an eighth segment of the fruit; a *wheel* is a whole slice of the fruit; a *slice* is half a wheel; a *peel* is a short piece of the peel or skin (a circular piece is best), gently curled in the middle (see Vodka Martini; no.9); and a *twist* is a thin slice of peel, twisted into a fine corkscrew shape (see Vodka Gimlet; no.18).

Cocktail Onions: These are Silverskin (small, white) onions, which come pickled in a jar. They are usually served by placing them loose in a drink or in a drink on a cocktail stick. Rinse before using unless otherwise stated in the recipe.

Cherries: Maraschino cherries are marasca cherries preserved in a jar of maraschino liqueur. They are usually dropped loose into the glass. When you are asked to garnish with a cherry, you need a maraschino cherry. Fresh cherries are sometimes used, too.

Cucumber: Cucumber sticks make great garnishes in refreshing cocktails. Simply cut a strip of cucumber, leaving the skin on for flavour, and place it in the glass.

Olives: These should be of the Queen Green variety. They can be placed loose in a drink, or on a cocktail stick. Always rinse before using unless otherwise specified.

Other Fruits: Fruits such as bananas, peaches, pineapples, raspberries, strawberries and watermelon are often used to decorate cocktails. Follow the garnish suggestions I have included in each recipe or go crazy and create some of your own.

Essential Equipment

There are some things that the mixologist just cannot do without – among them, the cocktail shaker, a corkscrew and a muddler. Here are just some of the most essential pieces of equipment you will need to make the cocktails in this book.

GENERAL

Let's start with the things you probably already have in your kitchen. A good "waiter's friend" is essential. This is a type of multi-vessel-opening device which has a flip-down corkscrew in the middle and a bottle opener on one end. A razor-sharp paring knife and chopping board are crucial for making your garnishes just as you want them, while a citrus squeezer will be useful for making sour mix (see p.17) and for small quantities of lemon, lime or orange juice used in the cocktails. A proper juicer will be really useful for making large quantities of fresh juices. You will certainly need a blender. An all-purpose kitchen blender will do, but be sure to crush ice cubes in a bag using a rolling pin before putting them in the blender (big lumps of ice can damage the motor) – better still invest in a proper ice-crusher. You probably already have ice tongs (for picking up ice cubes) – an ice scoop will be useful too for scooping up spoonfuls of crushed ice. A set of standard measuring spoons will almost certainly come in useful, although for a truly professional touch treat yourself to a set of shot measures. The basic rule for measuring out alcohol is to use the same system (equipment) for every ingredient – even if it is your general kitchen measuring jug – that way the proportions will always be equivalent. Finally, if you don't already have a lemon zester, consider buying one – it will be useful for peeling fine layers of zest from oranges, lemons and limes.

FOR SHAKING

The most important piece of equipment of all is the cocktail shaker. There are actually two types of shaker in common use today. The first, and easiest to use, is the standard three-piece shaker, which is made of stainless steel and consists of three separate parts: a tapered beaker, a close-fitting lid with a built-in strainer and a cap. The cocktail ingredients are simply placed in the beaker (when a method instructs to "shake with ice" the beaker should be two-thirds filled with ice), the strainer and the cap are fixed on and the mixture is shaken. If you are pouring the cocktail, the cap and lid are removed and the cocktail is poured into the glass. If the instructions are to "shake and strain", only the cap is removed, leaving the strainer in place while the drink is poured out. The other shaker available is the Boston Shaker, which has two pieces comprising a stainless steel beaker and a glass beaker which fit together snugly, enabling the contents to be shaken between them. An assertive tap on the side of the steel beaker is required to loosen the glass, then, if the drink is to be strained, you will need a separate coil-rimmed strainer which fixes to the steel beaker (you should probably invest in a strainer of this sort anyway).

FOR STIRRING

Of course, not all cocktails are shaken. Usually stirred cocktails are made in a mixing glass. Available in a range of sizes, these are simply sturdy glasses with a lip in which one or more servings can be mixed before being poured into a glass, or strained into it through a strainer. Some people stir in a cocktail jug – this has the added benefit of holding several servings at once. Find one with a good pouring lip (which can hold back ice cubes). If you don't want to invest in a jug or a glass just yet, you can use the base of your cocktail shaker, just be careful to hold back the ice if you need to.

To stir, the dedicated bar spoon – a flatish spoon, a little larger than a teaspoon in measure – is best. The long handle is essential for reaching to the bottom of the drink and, as the handles of most bar spoons are twisted with a flat disk at the end, they can be used for layering ingredients (see p.20) and muddling (see below), too.

MUDDLING

Resembling a mini-baseball bat, a muddler has a bulbous end and is similar to a pestle in its form and function. The tool is used to mash or crush any non-liquid ingredients (such as fruit, sugar cubes or herbs) before shaking or stirring. However, if you don't want to buy a muddler, a small wooden rolling pin will suffice. Muddling can be done in the beaker part of the shaker (or in a mixing glass if you have one).

Essential Techniques

Here are some of the most important techniques used in making and serving cocktails.

CHILLING, FROSTING AND WARMING A GLASS

Cocktails should be served in a chilled glass unless otherwise specified. The most effective way to chill a glass is to refrigerate it for an hour or two before use. Alternatively, fill the glass with ice topped up with water. Prepare your drink. When you are ready, simply empty the glass and pour in the cocktail. For cocktails that are served over ice, you can chill the glass by stirring the cocktail. However, this does change the properties of the drink – use only in emergencies! A frosted glass is basically a chilled glass that has a "frost" on the outside. The best way to achieve this effect is to put the glass in the freezer for thirty minutes or so before you use it. Hold the glass by the stem, so as not to make fingerprints in the frosting.

To warm a glass, place a bar spoon in the glass and fill the glass with hot water (the bar spoon will prevent the glass from cracking). Leave the glass for a minute or two and then discard the water and pour the cocktail into the glass. Remove the bar spoon last of all.

SHAKING, STIRRING AND BLENDING

Shaking some or all of the ingredients of a cocktail involves placing the ingredients in a cocktail shaker, often with a generous scoop of ice cubes, putting on the lid and shaking vigorously for several seconds. Make sure you have a firm grip of both ends of the shaker and never shake carbonated drinks as they are likely to explode.

To stir a cocktail, place the listed ingredients in a mixing glass or jug (or the uncapped base of your shaker) with a generous scoop of ice and stir with either end of a bar spoon for several seconds (aim to blend the flavours together without making the drink cloudy). Cocktails made with fizzy drinks need to be stirred just once or twice.

Blend a cocktail by putting all the ingredients (including the crushed ice) into a blender (see p.18) and whizzing until the contents are smooth.

STRAINING AND POURING

Drinks should be poured (including the ice) or strained (leaving the ice behind) as soon as they are made to retain maximum freshness and to avoid any unwanted dilution before they reach the glass. Always empty and dry out a cocktail shaker or mixing glass before making a fresh drink (even if you are making the same recipe), otherwise the delicate balance of ingredients will be upset by any residual melting ice.

LAYERING, FLOATING (pictured, near right) AND TOPPING

Layering is the method by which two or more spirits and/or liqueurs are poured into a glass to form layers floating on top of one another. Always pour the drinks into the glass in the order given in the recipe as this relates directly to the density of the ingredients (denser spirits first) and any variation will likely end up in a muddy mess. Pour each liquid in slowly and over the back of a spoon, or down the twisted handle and over the flat base of a bar spoon, to control the flow. Layered drinks are most commonly served in a shot glass. "Floating" is similar to layering, but this time only one ingredient floats on top of a mix of others. "Topping" (or "filling") simply means adding liquid (often soda or lemonade) to the mix to fill the drink to the top of the glass.

TWISTING (pictured, below centre)

To add a twist of something (usually lemon, orange or lime) to a drink, use a zester (see p.18) to remove a strip of the outer layer of the fruit's skin. Wind this slender strip of peel tightly around a drinking straw to create a coiled garnish to drape over the edge of the glass. A "loose twist" can be created by winding the peel loosely around the straw or around something with a larger circumference, such as the neck of a wine bottle.

SALTING AND SUGARING A GLASS (pictured, below right)

These terms refer to the technique of coating the rim of a glass, most commonly a Martini or Margarita glass, with salt or sugar for added taste. Wet the rim of the glass with a wedge of citrus fruit by running the juicy edge of the fruit over the rim of the glass. Then, dip the rim into a shallow saucer of granulated sugar or of salt. The rim should set almost immediately. For variation, you can also try dipping the glass rim into cocoa powder or nutmeg if you think it might suit the cocktail you are making. Some cocktails suggest using a small amount of liqueur instead of lime or lemon juice to help the sugar or salt stick (and to add an extra flavour to the cocktail during drinking). You can also try lining the rim of the glass with the fruit's peel for a subtle fruit flavour.

INFUSING

Various herbs, spices and fruits can be used to infuse spirits such as gin, vodka and rum. Infusing can be a fun way of experimenting with flavours to create your own variations of the cocktails in this book. Place a small quantity of the fruit, herb or spice in a bottle of the suggested spirit, seal it and leave for a week or two (the longer the better). To speed along the process, you can warm the prepared bottle (by placing it in a pan of just-boiled water) for around 30 minutes. Then, leave the alcohol to cool and open a day or two later. You'll be surprised at just how much flavour has infused into the spirit, changing its character substantially.

Cocktail Glasses

There are dozens of glasses available in which to serve cocktails, but for the purposes of this book I have chosen nine basic styles of glass, one of which will happily provide a suitable receptacle for every single one of the 365 cocktail recipes.

Classic versions of the nine glass styles are described and pictured below. (Each glass also has a drawn icon. These icons are used with the recipes to indicate the appropriate glass for serving.) Of course, there are many variations of each of the classic styles of glass (long stems, short stems; tapered bowls, conical bowls; and so on). These variations change with fasion and design, and many of them are pictured in the book. Generally speaking, I think that the more simple and classic the style of glass, the better the taste of the drink supped from it.

❶ ♍ Champagne Flute: A traditional long-stemmed flute is perfect for all champagne cocktails. The tall, tapered shape of the bowl helps to retain the champagne's bubbles, while the length of the stem provides plenty of room for holding the glass without the need to touch the bowl (your hands will unnecessarily warm the drink if you do this).

❷ ♀ Snifter: This large, round glass with a narrow neck and short stem is recognizable to many as the traditional brandy glass. It is used for drinking neat brandy and cognac and for most brandy-based cocktails. The short stem and large bowl are designed for cupping the drink in your hands to warm it.

❸ ♉ Martini: Probably the glass most identified with cocktails (sometimes called simply a "cocktail glass"). Hold on to the stem so as not to warm the drink with your hands.

❹ ⬚ Pilsner: The tall pilsner glass, which narrows from the top to the bottom, is traditionally used to serve lager. In the cocktail world it is also used for the famous Singapore Sling (see no.89) and other similar cocktails.

❺ ⬚ Margarita: Although many bars serve the Margarita in a martini glass, the cocktail does have a dedicated glass of its own (sometimes this kind of glass is known as a coupette). The extra-wide brim is perfect for salting (see p.21).

❻ ⬚ Shot: Used for small but intense ice-free cocktails, as well as single shots of liquor, these little glasses come in endless variations – just make sure they are sturdy if you intend to slam them.

❼ ⬚ Highball: A tall, straight-sided glass with a generous capacity, the highball is used for long drinks (lots of room for ice). Some long cocktails should strictly be served in a collins glass. This is similar to a highball but slightly taller and narrower. However, the highball will suffice for all the long drinks in this book. It is also probably the glass most commonly used in making cocktails.

❽ ⬚ Old-fashioned: A standard whiskey or bourbon glass, the old-fashioned is a tumbler (a short, sturdy glass) named after the classic cocktail (see no.211) first served in it. You may sometimes see it called a rocks glass as it is ideal for serving drinks (and cocktails) on the rocks.

❾ ⬚ Large Wine Glass: The idea of serving a cocktail in a wine glass might seem odd, but the large bowl is great for holding a lot of cocktail, while the long stem ensures that you can hold the drink without warming the glass in your hands.

❺   **❻**   **❼**   **❽**   **❾**

vodka

From its humble origins in medieval eastern Europe, vodka (a Russian word meaning "little water") has become one of the world's most popular spirits. First produced in Russia and Poland as long ago as the 12th century, vodka is a neutral-testing spirit which is traditionally made from rye, but can also be made from molasses and potato. Vodka became popular in the US and western Europe in the wake of World War II, when servicemen returned from overseas with precious bottles of the stuff.

After distillation the vodka is charcoal-filtered to remove every last trace of flavour and, apart from its fiery alcoholic kick, becomes not only tasteless, but odourless and colourless, too. This makes the spirit a mixologist's dream, as it combines effortlessly with any number of other ingredients. There are also many popular flavoured vodkas on the market, which are made by infusing regular vodka (see p.21) with a variety of fruits and spices, such as lemon, blackcurrant, pepper and vanilla.

001 watermelon martini

1 slice watermelon (large)
2 oz / 56 ml vodka
dash sugar syrup

GLASS TYPE: ♈ ⬭
ALCOHOL RATING: ●●○○○
STAR RATING: ★★★★★

Slice the watermelon flesh away from the rind. Discard the pips. Muddle the flesh in a shaker. Pour the vodka and sugar syrup into the shaker; shake all the ingredients together with ice and strain into a glass. To garnish, place a wedge of watermelon inside the glass.

Made right, this refreshing drink is my personal favourite: be sure to strain every drop of watermelon into the glass, there should be just enough mixture to fill the glass – no less and no more. This mix also makes a great shot.

002 black Russian

1 ½ oz / 42 ml vodka
¾ oz / 21 ml Kalúha
cola

GLASS TYPE: ⬭
ALCOHOL RATING: ●●◑○○
STAR RATING: ★★★☆☆

Pour the first 2 ingredients into a glass filled with ice. Top with cola.

A popular and definitive cocktail, this drink was served originally without the cola.

003 white Russian

2 oz / 56 ml vodka
1 oz / 28 ml Kalúha
milk or single cream

GLASS TYPE: ⬭
ALCOHOL RATING: ●●●○○
STAR RATING: ★★★☆☆

Shake the ingredients together with ice and strain into an ice-filled glass. Use sprinkles of cocoa powder or chocolate flakes to garnish.

This is another timeless cocktail and sister drink to the Black Russian (above). Try both milk and cream to give the drink a smoother taste.

004 Jericho's breeze

1 oz / 28 ml vodka
¾ oz / 21 ml blue curaçao
2 ½ oz / 70 ml sour mix (see p.17)
½ oz / 14 ml lime juice
splash orange juice
dash sugar syrup
splash lemonade

GLASS TYPE: ⬭
ALCOHOL RATING: ●●○○○
STAR RATING: ★★★☆☆

Pour all of the ingredients (except for the lemonade) into a shaker, shake and strain into a glass filled with crushed ice. Top with lemonade. Place a pineapple slice and a cherry inside the glass to garnish.

The combination of non-alcoholic ingredients contained in this mix means that this cocktail tastes less alcoholic than it is.

005 jungle juice

1 oz / 28 ml vodka
¾ oz / 21 ml rum
½ oz / 14 ml triple sec
1 oz / 28 ml cranberry juice
1 oz / 28 ml orange juice
1 oz / 28 ml pineapple juice
splash sour mix (see p.17)

GLASS TYPE: ▯
ALCOHOL RATING: ●●○○○
STAR RATING: ★★★☆☆

Pour all the ingredients into a glass filled with ice. Stir. Drop an orange slice
and a cherry into the glass to garnish.

*This is a diverse-tasting mix, and as you take each sip you will taste a little
of each flavour.*

006 caiprioska

5 lime wedges
3 tsp sugar (brown, granulated)
2 oz / 56 ml vodka

GLASS TYPE: ▯
ALCOHOL RATING: ●●○○○
STAR RATING: ★★★★☆

Muddle the lime together with the sugar in a sugar-rimmed old-fashioned
glass. Fill the glass with crushed ice and top with the vodka.

*This fine lime drink is a version of the Caipirinha (see no.174) – it's just that it's
made with vodka instead of cachaça.*

French martini

1 ½ oz / 42 ml vodka
¼ oz / 7 ml Chambord
1 ½ oz / 42 ml pineapple juice

GLASS TYPE: ▽
ALCOHOL RATING: ●●○○○
STAR RATING: ★★★☆☆

Shake all the ingredients together with ice and strain into the glass.
To garnish, place a pineapple leaf inside the glass.

*This cocktail was created in Harry's New York Bar, Paris. The mix of Chambord
and pineapple produces a sweet, easy-to-drink martini.*

008 Gid Barnett

1 oz / 28 ml vodka
½ oz / 14 ml blue curaçao
½ oz / 14 ml parfait amour
½ oz / 14 ml water (cold)
dash sugar syrup

GLASS TYPE: ▯
ALCOHOL RATING: ●●○○○
STAR RATING: ★★★☆☆

Shake all the ingredients together with ice and strain into a glass filled with
crushed ice. To garnish, dangle an orange twist over the rim of the glass.

*This cocktail was created by Gideon Barnett in 1998 for the patrons of Bill's Bar,
Tokyo. Gideon set the trend for including ½ oz/14 ml of water, which dilutes this
mix immediately. The idea is that rather than waiting for the ice to melt to make
the cocktail more palatable, drinking can commence straight away!*

about the vodka martini

The original martini, which was created in the US in the late 19th century, was made with a gin base (see no.59). However, the Vodka Martini is now a classic in its own right and, in all but the most traditional and old-fashioned cocktail bars, when you order a martini you will be given a Vodka Martini.

Following the arrival of vodka in the US and western Europe in the late 1940s, the current predilection for vodka over gin can largely be attributed to the popularity of the first James Bond movie *Dr No* in 1962 – the British spy James Bond is famously partial to a Vodka Martini, "shaken, not stirred", thus helping to bring the drink to an audience far beyond the exclusive cocktail lounges of New York, London and Paris.

However, purist Vodka Martini drinkers would never drink a shaken martini, preferring the traditional stirred version. Apart from the fact that a shaken martini is cloudy, it is also less alcoholic. Shaking the ingredients causes some of the alcohol to evaporate. Stirring merely chills the alcohol slightly. Usually, any olive used as a garnish must be rinsed so as not to pollute the drink with its brine. The exception to this is the Dirty Martini – martini ingredients mixed with a muddled olive – a popular variant of this most sophisticated of classic cocktails.

Extra Dry, Perfect and Sweet are the three most favoured variations on the traditional Dry Martini. To make a Perfect Martini or a Sweet Martini use the same method as you would for the traditional Dry Martini (see opposite), except that you should strain away half (rather than all) of the vermouth. To make an Extra Dry Martini, pour the vermouth into a chilled glass and swill it around to line the glass with vermouth. Dispense with the vermouth. Pour the vodka into a shaker filled with ice and stir until chilled. Strain into the vermouth-lined glass.

extra dry martini
2 oz / 56 ml vodka
¼ oz / 7 ml dry vermouth
Garnish with a curled lemon peel, and an olive if desired

perfect martini
2 oz / 56 ml vodka
¼ oz / 7 ml dry vermouth
¼ oz / 7 ml sweet vermouth
Garnish with a curled lemon or orange peel, and an olive if desired

sweet martini
2 oz / 56 ml vodka
½ oz / 14 ml sweet vermouth
Garnish with a curled orange peel

009 **vodka martini (dry)**
2 oz / 56 ml vodka
½ oz / 14 ml dry vermouth

GLASS TYPE: Y
ALCOHOL RATING: ●●◑○○
STAR RATING: ★★★★☆

Pour the vermouth into an ice-filled shaker to line the ice with vermouth. Strain all of the vermouth away. Pour the vodka into the shaker. Stir for a few seconds to chill the vodka. Strain into a chilled glass. Garnish with a curled lemon peel, and an olive if desired. If possible, pre-chill the vodka to minimize the dilution of alcohol when stirring.

010 blue lagoon

1 oz / 28 ml vodka
1 oz / 28 ml blue curaçao
lemonade

GLASS TYPE: ⬜
ALCOHOL RATING: ●●○○○
STAR RATING: ★★☆☆☆

Pour the first 2 ingredients into an ice-filled glass. Top with lemonade. Drop
in a cherry to garnish.

*The Blue Lagoon is believed to have been created around 1960 at Harry's New York
Bar, Paris. Try slipping a slice of pineapple inside the glass for extra zest.*

011 vodka sour

2 oz / 56 ml vodka
2 drops Angostura bitters
juice of ½ lemon
1 tsp powdered (caster) sugar
1 tsp egg white (optional)

GLASS TYPE: ⬜
ALCOHOL RATING: ●●○○○
STAR RATING: ★★★☆☆

Shake all the ingredients together with ice and strain into an ice-filled glass.
To garnish place a slice of lemon and a cherry in the drink.

*It's generally accepted that the best way to make a sour is with egg white, but
in the interest of public health (raw egg poses the risk of salmonella poisoning),
I have listed the egg white as optional.*

012 Caribbean cruise

1 oz / 28 ml vodka
¼ oz / 7 ml coconut rum
¼ oz / 7 ml light rum
splash grenadine
4 oz / 112 ml pineapple juice

GLASS TYPE: ⬜
ALCOHOL RATING: ●●○○○
STAR RATING: ★★★☆☆

Shake all the ingredients (except for the pineapple juice) with ice and strain
into an ice-filled glass. Top with pineapple juice. To garnish, place a wedge
of pineapple on the rim of the glass and float a cherry on top of the ice.

*Allow this drink to take you on a tropical cruise – think bright sunshine and
a refreshing breeze, even if you're in a dark and smoky bar!*

013 long grape

8 seedless green grapes (plus 3 for garnish)
2 oz / 56 ml blackcurrant vodka
dash sugar syrup
lemonade

GLASS TYPE: ⬜
ALCOHOL RATING: ●●○○○
STAR RATING: ★★★★★

Muddle the grapes in a shaker. Pour in the vodka and the sugar syrup.
Shake with ice and strain the mix into an ice-filled glass. Top with lemonade.
Drop 3 grapes (halved) into the glass to garnish.

*This was one of the first cocktails to use flavoured vodka. If you can't find
blackcurrant vodka, you can use regular vodka with a dash of blackcurrant syrup.*

014 sino-Soviet split

2 oz / 56 ml vodka
1 oz / 28 ml amaretto
dash milk or single cream

GLASS TYPE: ▢
ALCOHOL RATING: ●●●○○
STAR RATING: ★★★☆☆

Pour all of the ingredients into a glass filled with ice.
Try this one with a scoop of blended vanilla ice cream instead of the milk or cream.

015▼ purple passion tea

1 passion fruit (peeled)
¼ oz / 7 ml vodka
¼ oz / 7 ml gin
¼ oz / 7 ml light rum
½ oz / 14 ml Chambord
4 oz / 112 ml sour mix (see p.17)
¼ oz / 7 ml lime juice
3 oz / 84 ml lemonade

GLASS TYPE: ▢
ALCOHOL RATING: ●◐○○○
STAR RATING: ★★★★☆

Muddle the passion fruit in a shaker. Add the remaining ingredients (except for the lemonade). Shake with ice and pour into a glass. Top with lemonade.
This mix is a less alcoholic version of the original Long Island Iced Tea (see no 40)

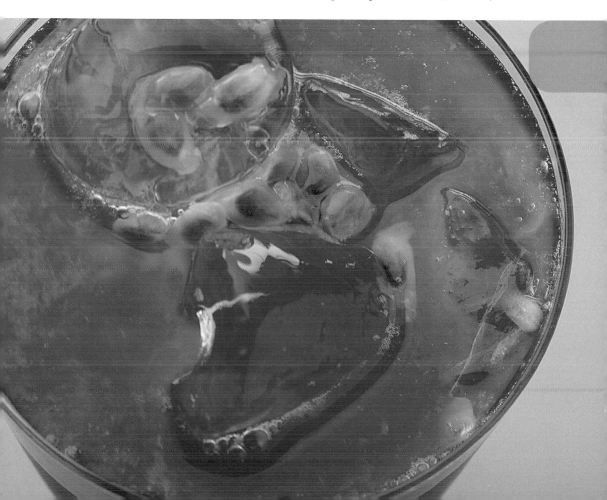

016   **WOO WOO**
1 oz / 28 ml vodka
½ oz / 14 ml peach schnapps
cranberry juice

GLASS TYPE: ⎕
ALCOHOL RATING: ●◐○○○
STAR RATING: ★★★☆☆

Pour the ingredients into a glass filled with ice. Stir. Put a lime wedge inside the glass to garnish.

This simple mix is a drier alternative to Sex on the Beach (see no.278).

017▼   **paradise martini**
2 oz / 56 ml vanilla vodka
1 oz / 28 ml strawberry purée
½ oz / 14 ml coconut milk
¼ oz / 7 ml orgeat syrup
dash sugar syrup

GLASS TYPE: 🍸
ALCOHOL RATING: ●●○○○
STAR RATING: ★★★★☆

Pour all of the ingredients into a shaker, shake with ice and strain into the glass. Place a whole strawberry on the rim of the glass to garnish.

This mix was created by Ben Pundle of the Sanderson Hotel, London. Vanilla vodka is new on the market – if you can't find any, you can use vanilla-infused vodka (see p.21).

018▲ vodka gimlet

1 ½ oz / 42 ml vodka
1 oz / 28 ml lime cordial
1 tsp powdered (caster) sugar (optional)

GLASS TYPE: ⏦ □
ALCOHOL RATING: ●◐○○○
STAR RATING: ★★★★★

Shake all the ingredients together with ice and strain into a martini glass.
Garnish with a tight lime twist. Alternatively, you can serve the Gimlet on
the rocks in an old-fashioned glass: fill the glass with ice and, as before,
shake with ice and strain the mix into the glass.

This is the vodka version of the gin Gimlet (see no.52). I love the crunch of sugar
served over ice – but you can use sugar syrup if you prefer a smoother texture.

019 headless horseman

2 oz / 56 ml vodka
3 dashes Angostura bitters
ginger ale

GLASS TYPE: □
ALCOHOL RATING: ●●○○○
STAR RATING: ★★☆☆☆

Pour the vodka and the bitters into a glass filled with ice and top with ginger
ale. Place a slice of orange inside the glass to garnish.

The Angostura bitters add a herbal flavour to this refreshing drink.

020 'Sisco Bay

1 ½ oz / 42 ml citrus vodka
4 oz / 112 ml sour mix (see p.17)
splash cranberry juice
splash orange juice
splash lemonade

GLASS TYPE: ☐
ALCOHOL RATING: ●◑○○○○
STAR RATING: ★★★☆☆

Pour the vodka, sour mix and cranberry juice into a shaker, shake with ice and strain into an ice-filled glass. Top with orange juice and lemonade. Place a slice of lemon inside the glass to garnish.

The sourness of this mix creates a fine pre-dinner drink.

021 velvet hammer

1 ½ oz / 42 ml vodka
1 tbsp crème de cacao (white)
1 tbsp single cream

GLASS TYPE: ▽
ALCOHOL RATING: ●◑○○○
STAR RATING: ★★★☆☆

Pour all of the ingredients into a shaker, shake with ice and strain into the glass. Garnish with sprinkles of cocoa powder.

Although many after-dinner drinks are made with cream, there's something to be said for making them the first drink of the evening – to line the stomach, of course.

022 velvet peach hammer

1 ¾ oz / 49 ml vodka
¾ oz / 21 ml peach schnapps
splash sour mix (see p.17)

GLASS TYPE: ☐ ☐
ALCOHOL RATING: ●●◑○○
STAR RATING: ★★★☆☆

Stir all the ingredients together with ice and strain into an ice-filled glass. Place a slice of peach inside the drink to garnish.

This drink also makes for a great shot – add an extra 1 oz/28 ml vodka. Shake and strain into a shot glass.

023 cosmopolitan

2 oz / 56 ml citrus vodka
1 oz / 28 ml triple sec
2 oz / 56 ml cranberry juice
dash lime juice

GLASS TYPE: ▽
ALCOHOL RATING: ●●●○○
STAR RATING: ★★★★★

Shake all the ingredients together with ice and strain into the glass. Garnish with a flamed orange peel. Hold the middle of the peel between thumb and forefinger above the glass and gently heat with a lighter flame. Ensure you direct the orange peel away from yourself, and use wax-free oranges or the peel's oil will burn black. While heating the peel, squeeze it to release the fruit's aromatic oils onto the surface of the drink. Drop in the peel.

Flaming the orange peel to release the oils of the fruit will enhance the citrus flavour of this drink, which is a fashionable and easy-to-drink variation on the Vodka Martini (see no.9). Popularized in New York during the 1980s, the Cosmopolitan was originally made with unflavoured vodka and garnished with a lime wedge.

about the Moscow mule

The origins of this long, refreshing drink with a mule-like kick and added ginger zing, lie not in the Russian capital but a world away, in a bar on Hollywood's Sunset Strip. In the 1940s the owner of the Cock 'n' Bull saloon, who had a sideline in ginger beer production, met a visiting businessman who happened to own Smirnoff vodka. Between them they came up with a cocktail which combined the two with a dash of lime. The drink was a huge hit. Traditionally served in a copper mug, the Moscow Mule is available today ready-mixed in copper-coloured bottles. However, nothing beats the self-mixed real thing.

Although ginger beer is available in both alcoholic and non-alcoholic forms, it is the non-alcoholic variety that should be used to make the Moscow Mule, and ginger beer should not be confused with the much sweeter, also non-alcoholic, ginger ale. Inspired by this cocktail, bartenders have used the recipe to mix other base spirits with ginger beer – bourbon or dark rum have proved to be especially popular alternatives to the vodka base.

024 **Moscow mule**
2 lime wedges (halved)
2 slices fresh ginger
1 tsp sugar (white, granulated)
1 ½ oz / 42 ml vodka
ginger beer

GLASS TYPE: 〔〕
ALCOHOL RATING: ●●○○○○
STAR RATING: ★★★★☆

Muddle the lime together with the ginger and the sugar in a shaker. Pour in the vodka and ginger beer. Shake with ice and strain into an ice-filled glass. Garnish with lime wedges and shredded ginger.

banana extravaganza

025

1 oz / 28 ml vodka
½ oz / 14 ml light rum
½ oz / 14 ml crème de banane
1 oz / 28 ml cranberry juice
1 oz / 28 ml orange juice
1 oz / 28 ml pineapple juice

GLASS TYPE: 🍸
ALCOHOL RATING: ●●○○○
STAR RATING: ★★★☆☆

Shake all the ingredients together with ice and strain into an ice-filled glass.
Place a slice of pineapple and a slice of lime inside the glass to garnish.
The mix of vodka and rum gives this banana cocktail quite a kick.

Madras

026

1 ½ oz / 42 ml vodka
4 oz / 112 ml cranberry juice
1 oz / 28 ml orange juice

GLASS TYPE: 🍸
ALCOHOL RATING: ●◐○○○
STAR RATING: ★★☆☆☆

Shake the ingredients together with ice and strain into an ice-filled glass.
Place a lime wedge inside the glass to garnish.
This mix of cranberry and orange creates a simple and timeless cocktail.

madraski

027

1 kiwi fruit (peeled)
1 ½ oz / 42 ml vodka
2 oz / 56 ml cranberry juice
1 oz / 28 ml orange juice

GLASS TYPE: 🍸
ALCOHOL RATING: ●●○○○
STAR RATING: ★★☆☆☆

Muddle the kiwi in a shaker and pour in the vodka, cranberry and orange.
Shake all the ingredients together with ice and strain into an ice-filled glass.
Place a peeled slice of kiwi on the rim of the glass to garnish.
The addition of kiwi makes this cocktail a fresh-fruit version of the Madras (above).

English tea

028

2 oz / 56 ml vodka
6 oz / 168 ml Earl Grey tea (cold)
1 oz / 28 ml lemon juice
dash sugar syrup
2 mint leaves

GLASS TYPE: 🍸
ALCOHOL RATING: ●●○○○
STAR RATING: ★★★☆☆

Shake all the ingredients together with ice. Strain the mix into an ice-filled
glass. To garnish, put a lemon twist inside the glass and a sprig of mint
on top of the ice.
The Earl Grey tea gives this drink a particularly delicate and fragrant flavour.
However, you can use ordinary tea if you prefer.

029▲ cappuccino cocktail

¾ oz / 21 ml vodka
¾ oz / 21 ml Kalúha
a single espresso (hot)
¾ oz / 21 ml single cream
dash sugar syrup

GLASS TYPE: 🍸 ▯
ALCOHOL RATING: ●◐○○○
STAR RATING: ★★★★☆

Pour all of the ingredients into a shaker, shake and strain into a martini glass. Use sprinkles of cocoa powder or chocolate flakes to garnish.
The best way to be woken up – well almost! Be warned, too many may cause a caffeine overload. This cocktail also makes a good shot.

030 vodka grasshopper

¾ oz / 21 ml vodka
¾ oz / 21 ml crème de cacao (white)
¾ oz / 21 ml crème de menthe (green)

GLASS TYPE: ▯
ALCOHOL RATING: ●●◐○○
STAR RATING: ★☆☆☆☆

Shake the ingredients together with ice and strain into a glass filled with crushed ice. Put a sprig of mint inside the glass to garnish.
I'm not a lover of crème de menthe – but if you are, you'll enjoy this one.

about the bloody Mary

Renowned by many as a good hangover cure, this distinctive classic cocktail is thought to have been created at Harry's New York Bar in Paris in the 1920s and is popularly believed to have been named after Queen Mary Tudor of England, whose ruthless persecution of Protestants during her short reign (1553–1558) earned her the nickname "Bloody Mary".

The Bloody Mary originally tended to be presented in a themed glass in the shape of a cockerel or a boat, but in today's bars the drink is usually served in a highball. There is much passionate debate among bartenders as to what constitutes the perfect Bloody Mary. Of all the classic cocktails, this cocktail can be most easily tailored to the individual drinker's specific tastes and there are many variations. Increasingly, up-market bars like to create their own gourmet tomato pastes to add to their own fresh tomato juice. These pastes may be mixed with myriad different herbs, such as rosemary and basil. Some better-known variations of the Bloody Mary include the addition of clam juice or beef extract to the mix. Experiment to create your own personal classic by adding or subtracting any number of the Bloody Mary's secondary ingredients (the vodka and tomato juice are essential): add some avocado for a Mexican flavour, or try Wasabi (a Japanese spice) instead of horseradish for a hint of the East – the possibilities are endless!

bloody Mary
1 ½ oz / 42 ml vodka
4 oz / 112 ml tomato juice
½ tsp horseradish
½ tsp Worcestershire sauce
2 or 3 drops Tabasco sauce
dash lemon juice
salt and pepper to taste

GLASS TYPE: []
ALCOHOL RATING: ●◐○○○
STAR RATING: ★★★★☆

Shake all the ingredients together with ice and strain into an ice-filled glass. Garnish with a slice of lemon or lime, a stick of celery and cracked black pepper.

032   bloody Mary no. 2

1 ½ oz / 42 ml vodka
dash red wine
4 oz / 112 ml tomato juice
½ tsp horseradish
½ tsp Worcestershire sauce
2 or 3 drops Tabasco sauce
dash lemon juice
2 basil leaves
salt and pepper to taste
½ oz / 14 ml white sherry

GLASS TYPE: ▯
ALCOHOL RATING: ●●●○○
STAR RATING: ★★★★★

Shake all the ingredients (except for the sherry) together with ice and strain into an ice-filled glass. Float the sherry on top. Garnish with a slice of lemon, a stick of celery, 2 bay leaves, 1 cherry tomato (halved) and cracked black pepper.

Another fantastic hangover cure. But be warned – the addition of wine and sherry makes this cocktail a more lethal version of the classic Bloody Mary (see no.31).

033   lychee martini

2 oz / 56 ml vodka
3 oz / 84 ml lychee syrup
dash sugar syrup

GLASS TYPE: ▼
ALCOHOL RATING: ●●○○○
STAR RATING: ★★★★☆

Shake the ingredients together with ice and strain into the glass. Garnish with 2 tinned lychees on a 3-inch/75-mm cocktail skewer.

I first made this drink working at the Sanderson Hotel in London – it was probably the most popular drink for our female clients. The lychee syrup comes from a tin of lychees, which you can buy in most supermarkets.

034   Polynesian

1 ½ oz / 42 ml vodka
¾ oz / 21 ml cherry brandy
juice of 1 lime

GLASS TYPE: ▼
ALCOHOL RATING: ●●◐○○
STAR RATING: ★★★☆☆

Pour all the ingredients into a shaker, shake and strain into a sugar-rimmed glass. Dangle a lime twist over the rim of the glass to garnish.

These ingredients complement each other perfectly.

035   Georgia peach

1 ½ oz / 42 ml vodka
½ oz / 14 ml peach schnapps
dash grenadine
lemonade

GLASS TYPE: ▯
ALCOHOL RATING: ●●○○○
STAR RATING: ★★☆☆☆

Pour all the ingredients (except for the lemonade) into a glass filled with ice. Top with lemonade. Put a slice of peach inside the glass to garnish.

This cocktail has a deep peach taste and it's designed to be sipped slowly.

036 **L.A. sunrise**
1 oz / 28 ml vodka
½ oz / 14 ml crème de banane
2 oz / 56 ml orange juice
2 oz / 56 ml pineapple juice
¼ oz / 7 ml light rum

GLASS TYPE:
ALCOHOL RATING: ●●○○○
STAR RATING: ★★★☆☆

Pour all the ingredients (except for the rum) into a glass filled with ice. Stir. Float the rum on the top. To decorate, place an orange wheel on the rim of the glass and drop a cherry into the drink.
If you like banana then this is a cocktail for you. Try replacing the fruit juice with fresh fruit and blending all the ingredients together for a real treat.

037 **Harvey Wallbanger**
1 oz / 28 ml vodka
4 oz / 112 ml orange juice
½ oz / 14 ml Galliano

GLASS TYPE:
ALCOHOL RATING: ●●○○○
STAR RATING: ★★★☆☆

Pour the vodka and the orange juice into a glass filled with ice. Stir. Float the Galliano on top. Place a slice of orange inside the glass to garnish.
The popular story behind the name of this drink is that a '60s Manhattan surfer, named Harvey, used to celebrate surfing wins with his signature mix of vodka, orange juice and Galliano. One victorious day he began to bang his surfboard against the walls of the bar, and this renowned cocktail was named.

038 **vodka sling**
2 oz / 56 ml vodka
juice of ½ lemon
1 tsp powdered (caster) sugar
soda

GLASS TYPE:
ALCOHOL RATING: ●●○○○
STAR RATING: ★★☆☆☆

Pour the first 3 ingredients into a glass filled with ice. Stir until the sugar has dissolved. Top with soda and stir again. Place a slice of lemon inside the glass to garnish.
Chic and simple – this is the vodka version of the Gin Sling (see no.90).

039 **vodka collins**
2 oz / 56 ml vodka
juice of ½ lemon
dash sugar syrup
soda

GLASS TYPE:
ALCOHOL RATING: ●●○○○
STAR RATING: ★★★★★

Shake the first 3 ingredients together with ice and strain into an ice-filled glass. Fill with soda. Place a slice of lemon inside the glass to garnish.
This cocktail derives from the gin-based Tom Collins (see no.57).

Long Island iced tea

½ oz / 14 ml vodka
½ oz / 14 ml gin
½ oz / 14 ml light rum
½ oz / 14 ml tequila
½ oz / 14 ml triple sec
juice of ¼ lemon
dash cola

GLASS TYPE: ▯
ALCOHOL RATING: ●●●○○
STAR RATING: ★★★★★

Shake all the ingredients (except for the cola) together with ice and strain into an ice-filled glass. Add the cola for colour and put a lemon wheel inside the glass to garnish.

TRADITIONAL CLASSIC

about the Long Island iced tea

Long Island Iced Tea — charming title, fearsome reputation. As its name would suggest, the drink was invented on Long Island, New York, probably during Prohibition when bartenders mixed any number and variety of bootleg spirits and coloured them with cola to make a cocktail that looked like an innocent iced tea. Today, the word "tea" is used as a generic term, meaning any long mixed drink comprising at least two clear spirits, served in a higball filled with ice.

This is a great popular classic — a favourite with groups of young drinkers in noisy bars gearing up for a night on the town. Beware of two things: first, that you get what you pay for. This cocktail should be an opaque, pale brown colour. If it looks dark brown in colour, there is too much cola in it and, consequently, less alcohol. Second, the combination of five different spirits means the Long Island Iced Tea is a powerfully strong cocktail, yet it is very easy to drink — drink it too fast (or drink too many) and you will be guaranteed a huge hangover. In moderation, however, this cocktail can make a fine start to a fun evening.

041 sea breeze

1 ½ oz / 42 ml vodka
4 oz / 112 ml cranberry juice
1 oz / 28 ml grapefruit juice

GLASS TYPE: ⛾
ALCOHOL RATING: ●◐○○○
STAR RATING: ★★★☆☆

Pour 1 oz/28 ml of the vodka and all the cranberry juice into an ice-filled glass. Pour the remaining vodka and the grapefruit juice into a shaker; shake with ice and strain into the mix. Put a lime slice inside the glass to garnish.

Topping the drink with the shaken vodka and grapefruit juice will give it a lovely foamy head. This bitter mix is quick to make – it's most popular in bars with fewer cocktails on their menu.

042 citronella cooler

1 oz / 28 ml citrus vodka
2 oz / 56 ml lemonade
1 oz / 28 ml cranberry juice
dash lime juice

GLASS TYPE: ⛾
ALCOHOL RATING: ●○○○○
STAR RATING: ★★☆☆☆

Pour all the ingredients into a glass filled with ice and drop in a lime wedge to garnish.

This cocktail tastes like a soft drink with a citrus zing – to help you reach maximum chill-out on a hot summer's day.

043 naked pretzel

¾ oz / 21 ml vodka
1 oz / 28 ml Midori
½ oz / 14 ml crème de cassis
2 oz / 56 ml pineapple juice

GLASS TYPE: ⛾
ALCOHOL RATING: ●●○○○
STAR RATING: ★★☆☆☆

Pour all of the ingredients into a glass filled with ice and stir. Put a pineapple slice and a pineapple leaf inside the glass to garnish.

This cocktail was invented by a bartender friend of mine, but I've never been able to find out the origins of its name.

044 bloody bull

1 oz / 28 ml vodka
2 oz / 56 ml tomato juice
½ oz / 14 ml lemon juice
2 oz / 56 ml beef bouillon (cubes)

GLASS TYPE: ⛾
ALCOHOL RATING: ●○○○○
STAR RATING: ★★★☆☆

Pour the vodka, tomato juice and lemon juice into a glass filled with ice. Add the beef bouillon and stir until the cubes have dissolved and the mixture is smooth. Garnish with a slice of lime.

From Mary to the Bull, and all you have to do is add beef. If you're feeling adventurous, try blending all the ingredients together with a handful of cherry tomatoes and ice. Spice with salt, pepper, basil, and even a pinch of coriander if desired. Serve the mixture chilled as a soup.

gin

The earliest records of gin production originate from 17th-century Holland, where a medicinal drink known as "genever" (the Dutch word meaning juniper) was distilled from grain and flavoured with juniper berries. However, mass production of the spirit for social drinking almost certainly originates from England (and particularly London). There, Dutch-born William of Orange (who acceded to the English throne in 1689) openly encouraged the distillation of English spirits, while at the same time raising import duty on spirits from France. Frequently blamed for drunkenness on the streets of London, gin was the drink of the poor until the levying of heavy distillation taxes forced only the most refined (and expensive) versions into production.

Today, gin's distinctive taste comes from the addition of natural flavourings, usually during a second distillation in a "carterhead pot still". These flavourings, along with juniper itself, are known as the "botanicals" and can include herbs, spices and fruit such as coriander, angelica, cinnamon, caraway seeds and orange. The precise blend of flavours will depend entirely on the producer.

045 Pollyanna

3 slices orange
3 slices pineapple
2 oz / 56 ml gin
½ oz / 14 ml sweet vermouth
½ tsp grenadine

GLASS TYPE: ♈
ALCOHOL RATING: ●●●○○
STAR RATING: ★★★★☆

Muddle the fruit in a shaker. Add the remaining ingredients, shake with ice and strain into the glass.

Fresh fruit pieces in a cocktail are a personal favourite for me – they cut through the alcohol to add a distinct, fruity tang; and they give the drink an extra-special appearance.

046 Monte Carlo imperial highball

2 oz / 56 ml gin
½ oz / 14 ml crème de menthe (white)
juice of ¼ lemon
champagne

GLASS TYPE: ▯
ALCOHOL RATING: ●●●○○
STAR RATING: ★★★☆☆

Shake all of the ingredients (except for the champagne) together with ice, and pour the mix into the glass. Fill the glass with champagne and stir.

This is one of the few highballs mixed with champagne. Usually, champagne cocktails are served in flutes without ice, as bartenders often view mixing champagne with ice as wasteful.

047 gin smash

1 sugar cube (white)
4 sprigs mint
2 oz / 56 ml gin
1 oz / 28 ml soda

GLASS TYPE: ▯
ALCOHOL RATING: ●●○○○
STAR RATING: ★★★☆☆

Muddle the sugar together with the mint in an old-fashioned glass. Add crushed ice and pour in the gin. Top with soda and stir. Drop in a cherry to garnish.

Whatever you do please don't be tempted to substitute the fresh mint with crème de menthe – it won't do the drink justice.

048 star daisy

1 oz / 28 ml gin
1 oz / 28 ml applejack or calvados
juice of ½ lemon
1 tsp grenadine
½ tsp powdered (caster) sugar

GLASS TYPE: ▯
ALCOHOL RATING: ●●○○○
STAR RATING: ★★★★☆

Shake all the ingredients with ice and strain into a glass. Add an ice cube. Put 2 slices of lemon and 2 slices of green apple, and even a cherry if desired, into the glass to garnish.

If this drink is too strong for your palate, you can dilute it with some soda.

049 grand royal fizz

2 oz / 56 ml gin
½ tsp maraschino
juice of ½ lemon
juice of ½ orange
2 tsp single cream
1 tsp powdered (caster) sugar
soda

GLASS TYPE: 🥛
ALCOHOL RATING: ●●○○○
STAR RATING: ★★☆☆☆

Shake all the ingredients (except for the soda) together with ice. Strain
the mix into an ice-filled glass. Fill with soda and stir.
*Take care not to over-do the cream – too much will take away the flavour
of the drink.*

050 delmonico

¾ oz / 21 ml gin
½ oz / 14 ml brandy
½ oz / 14 ml dry vermouth
½ oz / 14 ml sweet vermouth

GLASS TYPE: 🍸
ALCOHOL RATING: ●●◐○○
STAR RATING: ★★★☆☆

Stir all the ingredients together with ice in a shaker. Strain the mix into
a glass. Drop in a cherry to garnish.
*The juniper flavours of the gin are enhanced by the vermouth and sweetened by the
brandy to form a refined apéritif, which I think tastes great with a cigar!*

051 leave-it-to-me

1 ½ oz / 42 ml gin
¼ tsp maraschino
1 tsp lemon juice
1 tsp raspberry syrup

GLASS TYPE: 🍸
ALCOHOL RATING: ●●○○○
PERSONAL RATING: ★★★☆☆

Pour all of the ingredients into a shaker. Stir with ice. Strain the mix into
the glass.
*You can use raspberry purée instead of raspberry syrup (see pp.16–17) to give this
cocktail more texture. However, purée has a more subtle flavour than syrup, so you
may also wish to use a dash of raspberry liqueur to enhance the taste.*

052 gimlet

1 ½ oz / 42 ml gin
1 oz / 28 ml lime cordial

GLASS TYPE: 🍸 🥃
ALCOHOL RATING: ●◐○○○
STAR RATING: ★★★★☆

Shake the ingredients together with ice and strain into a martini glass.
Place a tight lime twist inside the glass to garnish. Alternatively, pour the
ingredients into an old-fashioned glass filled with ice. Garnish as before.
*The famous gin Gimlet is thought to have originated in the British Navy, taking its
name from the 18th-century tool used to tap barrels. The lime cordial balances
this sharp-tasting drink, which begins sour and finishes sweet. (See no.18 for the
Vodka Gimlet.)*

053   hula-hula

1 ½ oz / 42 ml gin
¾ oz / 21 ml orange juice
¼ tsp powdered (caster) sugar

GLASS TYPE: ♈
ALCOHOL RATING: ●○○○○
STAR RATING: ★★★★☆

Shake all of the ingredients together with ice and strain into the glass.
*For a sweeter option try this one rimmed with sugar. As you drink work your
way around the rim of the glass, tasting the sugar before you take each sip.*

054▼   blue devil

1 oz / 28 ml gin
½ tsp blue curaçao
1 tbsp maraschino
juice of 1 lime or ½ lemon

GLASS TYPE: ♈
ALCOHOL RATING: ●◑○○○
STAR RATING: ★★☆☆☆

Shake the ingredients together with ice and strain the mix into the glass.
Drop in a maraschino cherry to garnish.
*The blue curaçao makes this drink go blue but, despite its name and appearance,
the cocktail tastes of oranges because curaçao is an orange-flavoured liqueur.*

055 ▲ English rose

1 ½ oz / 42 ml gin
¾ oz / 21 ml apricot brandy
¾ oz / 21 ml dry vermouth
1 tsp grenadine
¼ tsp lemon juice

GLASS TYPE: ▽
ALCOHOL RATING: ●●●○○
STAR RATING: ★★★★★

Shake all of the ingredients together with ice and strain into a sugar-rimmed glass. Attach 2 fresh cherries to the rim of the glass for decoration.

The exquisite pink tones of this cocktail are reminiscent of a beautiful English rose.

056 flamingo

1 ½ oz / 42 ml gin
½ oz / 14 ml apricot brandy
juice of ½ lime
1 tsp grenadine

GLASS TYPE: ▽
ALCOHOL RATING: ●●○○○
STAR RATING: ★★★☆☆

Shake all the ingredients together with ice and strain into a glass. Dangle a loose lime twist over the rim of the glass to garnish.

This is a sweet and slightly sour-tasting cocktail.

about the Tom Collins

A "Collins" has become a generic term for any spirit-based cocktail made with lemon juice, sugar syrup and soda, hence the Brandy Collins, Rum Collins and Vodka Collins to name but three. However, its origins reputedly date back more than one hundred years, when the original gin-based drink, the Tom Collins, was first given its name. The story goes that a London bartender named John Collins first created the cocktail using Dutch Genever gin – a gin sweetened with sugar and glycerine, and one far more commonly available at the end of the 19th century than it is today. Genever gin was also known as "Old Tom", and so the drink created by John Collins rather confusedly became the Tom Collins. These days the two names have become almost interchangeable. However, if you are ordering the drink in a bar, always check the ingredients list or qualify which spirit base you are expecting – in some cocktail menus a John Collins is the name given to a whiskey-based drink (see no.212) while the Tom Collins remains its gin-based brother.

The Tom Collins is both a very popular and an incredibly classy drink. A tall, refreshing blend that masks an alcoholic kick, the cocktail seems most at home being idly enjoyed on hot summer's days.

057 **Tom Collins**

2 oz / 56 ml gin
juice of ½ lemon
1 tsp powdered (caster) sugar
soda

GLASS TYPE: 🍸🥃
ALCOHOL RATING: ●●○○○
STAR RATING: ★★★★★

Shake the first 3 ingredients together with ice and strain into an ice-filled glass. Fill with soda and stir. Garnish with an orange slice and a cherry.

058   western rose

1 oz / 28 ml gin
½ oz / 14 ml apricot brandy
½ oz / 14 ml dry vermouth
¼ tsp lemon juice

GLASS TYPE: Y
ALCOHOL RATING: ●●○○○
STAR RATING: ★★★☆☆

Shake all the ingredients together with ice and strain into the glass.
This cocktail is not as sweet as the English Rose (see no.55) as it has no grenadine in it. You can personalize the drink by substituting the apricot brandy with the liqueur of your choice, such as crème de framboises or crème de mûre.

059   gin martini

2 oz / 56 ml gin
½ oz / 14 ml dry vermouth

GLASS TYPE: Y
ALCOHOL RATING: ●●○○○
STAR RATING: ★★★☆☆

Pour the vermouth into an ice-filled shaker to line the ice with vermouth. Strain all of the vermouth away. Pour the gin into the shaker. Stir for a few seconds to chill the gin. Strain into a chilled glass. Garnish with a curled lemon peel, and an olive if desired.
Some purists argue that this is the only way to make a martini. However, although originally made with gin, the martini is now more commonly made with vodka (see no.9) – and personally I prefer vodka.

060   papaya sling

1 ½ oz / 42 ml gin
dash Angostura bitters
juice of 1 lime
1 tbsp papaya syrup
soda

GLASS TYPE: ▯
ALCOHOL RATING: ●◐○○○
STAR RATING: ★★★★☆

Shake all the ingredients (except for the soda) together with ice and strain into a glass filled with ice. Fill with soda and stir. To garnish, put a pineapple stick inside the glass.
The papaya is a sweet and bitter fruit (sweetest in the middle and more bitter toward the outside), which has a complementary taste when drunk with gin.

061   floradora cooler

2 oz / 56 ml soda or ginger ale
juice of 1 lime
1 tbsp grenadine
½ tsp powdered (caster) sugar
2 oz / 56 ml gin

GLASS TYPE: ▯
ALCOHOL RATING: ●●○○○
STAR RATING: ★★★☆☆

Pour 1 ½ oz/42 ml soda or ginger ale, the lime juice, the grenadine and the sugar into a highball. Stir. Fill the glass with ice and pour in the gin. Fill with the remaining soda or ginger ale and stir again. Place a lime twist inside the glass to garnish.
If you prefer a sweeter mix, opt for the ginger ale rather than the soda.

062 **shady grove**
1 ½ oz / 42 ml gin
juice of ½ lemon
1 tsp powdered (caster) sugar
ginger ale

GLASS TYPE:
ALCOHOL RATING: ●◐○○○
STAR RATING: ★★★★☆

Shake all the ingredients (except for the ginger ale) with ice. Strain the mix into an ice-filled highball and top with ginger ale. To garnish, place 3 slices of fresh ginger inside the glass.

For a non-fizzy version, try this with fresh ginger. Pour the first 3 ingredients into a shaker. Add a stick of fresh ginger. Shake with ice and strain into a martini glass.

063 **cream fizz**
2 oz / 56 ml gin
juice of ½ lemon
1 tsp single cream
1 tsp powdered (caster) sugar
soda

GLASS TYPE:
ALCOHOL RATING: ●●○○○
STAR RATING: ★★☆☆☆

Shake all the ingredients (except for the soda) together with ice and pour into the glass. Top with soda. Place a mint leaf inside the glass to garnish.

Be sure to shake this one vigorously for about 30 seconds – to the point where the ice becomes cracked. Once the mix is poured into the glass, a layer of cracked ice will form on the top of your drink.

064 **Hudson Bay**
1 oz / 28 ml gin
½ oz / 14 ml cherry brandy
1 ½ tsp 151-proof rum
1 tbsp orange juice
1 ½ tsp lime juice

GLASS TYPE:
ALCOHOL RATING: ●●●○○
STAR RATING: ★★★☆☆

Shake all the ingredients together with ice and strain into a glass.

Lost and found – I recently rediscovered this great (and rather strong!) mix.

065 **typhoon**
1 oz / 28 ml gin
½ oz / 14 ml Pernod
juice of ½ lime
champagne

GLASS TYPE:
ALCOHOL RATING: ●●◐○○
STAR RATING: ★★★☆☆

Shake all of the ingredients (except for the champagne) together with ice. Strain into an ice-filled glass. Top with champagne.

This is another champagne cocktail served in a highball (see no.46). The Pernod can be quite overpowering and it needs the ice to defuse it.

free silver

066

1 ½ oz / 42 ml gin
½ oz / 14 ml dark rum
juice of ¼ lemon
1 tbsp milk
½ tsp powdered (caster) sugar
soda

GLASS TYPE: 🍸
ALCOHOL RATING: ●●○○○
STAR RATING: ★★★☆☆

Shake all of the ingredients (except for the soda) together with ice and strain into an ice-filled glass. Top with soda.

Have you heard of the comic superhero, the Silver Surfer? I always think of him when I mix this drink – he wouldn't be able to save the world after one of these!

gin sangaree

067

½ tsp powdered (caster) sugar
1 tsp water
2 oz / 56 ml gin
dash passion fruit juice
dash soda
½ oz / 14 ml port

GLASS TYPE: 🍸
ALCOHOL RATING: ●●○○○
STAR RATING: ★★★☆☆

Pour the sugar and the water into a shaker, stir until the sugar is dissolved. Add the gin and stir. Pour into an ice-filled glass. Add the passion fruit and soda. Stir. Float the port on top. Garnish with nutmeg and a cinnamon stick.

To create a more fruity flavour, try squeezing the juice from a wedge of orange into the drink, and then drop the wedge inside the glass.

Hokkaido

068

1 ½ oz / 42 ml gin
1 oz / 28 ml sake
½ oz / 14 ml triple sec

GLASS TYPE: 🍸
ALCOHOL RATING: ●●●○○
STAR RATING: ★★★★★

Shake the ingredients with ice and strain into the glass.

Sake is a Japanese rice "wine" (although actually it is brewed like beer, using rice, water and yeast), traditionally drunk warm in cups after a meal. For a stronger sake-tasting cocktail, try mixing the Hokkaido with vodka (instead of the gin) and a little sugar syrup.

Parisian

069

1 oz / 28 ml gin
1 oz / 28 ml dry vermouth
¼ oz / 7 ml crème de cassis

GLASS TYPE: 🍸
ALCOHOL RATING: ●●○○○
STAR RATING: ★★★☆☆

Shake the ingredients together with ice and strain into the glass.

This is a delicious blackcurrant-flavoured cocktail.

gin Aloha

1 ½ oz / 42 ml gin
1 ½ oz / 42 ml triple sec
dash orange bitters
1 tbsp pineapple juice

GLASS TYPE: ᵧ
ALCOHOL RATING: ●●●○○
STAR RATING: ★★☆☆☆

Shake all the ingredients together with ice and strain into the glass.
Garnish with a pineapple leaf.
The orange bitters helps to bring out the sharpness of the pineapple in this mix of
gin and juice.

Wembley

1 ½ oz / 42 ml gin
¾ oz / 21 ml dry vermouth
½ tsp apple schnapps
¼ tsp apricot brandy

GLASS TYPE: ᵧ
ALCOHOL RATING: ●●●○○
STAR RATING: ★★★☆☆

Pour all the ingredients into a shaker, stir with ice and strain into the glass.
I'm told that this was the cocktail of choice during the UK's FA (Football Association)
soccer finals, which until 2000 were played at Wembley stadium in London.

about the Negroni

The Negroni is a sharp, quite bitter-tasting drink based on the colourful Italian apéritif, Campari. The cocktail is said to have been named by a 1920s bartender, Fosco Scarelli. A local Florentine count, Conte Camillo Negroni, decided one day to modify his favourite cocktail the Americano (which is made with Campari and vermouth alone; see cocktail no.295) to please his own taste for a drier drink with more bite. He was so delighted with the results that every time he went into Scarelli's bar he ordered the new mix. Quite naturally, Scarelli felt that the only name suitable for the cocktail was Negroni, after its creator.

The drink is traditionally made with sweet vermouth, but you can try it with sweet or dry according to your preference. Some drinkers prefer the Negroni garnished with orange instead of lemon, which gives a tang that reduces some of its bitter tones. You could even add a dash of sugar syrup to soften the drink's bite. In bars, it can be safer to qualify your preference for a gin-based Negroni, as it is becoming increasingly popular to make the drink with vodka instead of gin.

Negroni

¾ oz / 21 ml gin
¾ oz/ 21 ml Campari
¾ oz / 21 ml sweet or dry vermouth
soda (optional)

GLASS TYPE: ⬭
ALCOHOL RATING: ●●○○○
STAR RATING: ★★★★☆

Pour the first 3 ingredients into an old-fashioned glass filled with ice
and stir. Top with soda, if desired. Garnish with a slice of lemon and
a lemon twist.

tropical special

1 ½ oz / 42 ml gin
½ oz / 14 ml triple sec
2 oz / 56 ml grapefruit juice
1 oz / 28 ml lime juice
1 oz / 28 ml orange juice

GLASS TYPE: 🥃
ALCOHOL RATING: ●●○○○
STAR RATING: ★★★☆☆

Pour all the ingredients into a shaker, shake with ice and strain the mix into an ice-filled glass. To garnish put 2 slices of lime, 2 slices of orange and a cherry into the drink and mix the fruit in between the ice.
Triple sec is not often used in gin-based drinks. However, in this particular mix it really helps to enhance the flavour of the orange juice.

Park Avenue

1 ½ oz / 42 ml gin
¾ oz / 21 ml sweet vermouth
1 tbsp pineapple juice

GLASS TYPE: 🍸
ALCOHOL RATING: ●●○○○
STAR RATING: ★★★☆☆

Pour the ingredients into a shaker, stir with ice and strain into the glass.
As an alternative, try shaking the ingredients together with ice – this will give the drink a beautiful frothy head, and it won't be as strong as the stirred version.

ideal cocktail

1 oz / 28 ml gin
1 oz / 28 ml dry vermouth
¼ tsp maraschino
½ tsp grapefruit or lemon juice

GLASS TYPE: 🍸
ALCOHOL RATING: ●●○○○
STAR RATING: ★★☆☆☆

Shake all the ingredients together with ice and strain into the glass. Drop in a cherry to garnish.
Grapefruit will give this cocktail a tangy bite, while lemon will give it a sour-tasting edge – it's your choice.

cherry slipper

1 ½ oz / 42 ml gin
½ oz / 14 ml cherry brandy
½ oz / 14 ml madeira
1 tsp orange juice

GLASS TYPE: 🍸
ALCOHOL RATING: ●●○○○
STAR RATING: ★★★☆☆

Shake all the ingredients together with ice and strain into the glass. Place a twisted orange peel inside the glass to garnish.
Madeira is a fortified wine produced on the island of Madeira, off the coast of Morocco. Matured in heated casks, madeira has a distinctive caramel tang. For an orangey version of this cocktail, use triple sec instead of the wine. Be aware that this will increase the alcoholic content – triple sec is higher proof than madeira.

about the Bronx

Believed to have been invented in 1906 by bartender Jonny Solon at the Old Waldorf-Astoria bar in New York, the Bronx is said to have been named after Bronx Zoo (rather than the New York borough as we might assume). Solon believed that if you drink too many of this cocktail you are sure to hallucinate – and perhaps you might see strange and wonderful beasts, just like those he'd seen on a daytrip to the zoo.

The story goes that Solon created the cocktail in response to a challenge by a Waldorf restaurant customer. The customer sent his waiter over to Solon with the claim that the bartender wasn't able to invent anything new or interesting. Incensed, Solon told the waiter that he would prove the customer wrong. Solon mixed his new drink and gave it to the waiter to taste. It is said that the waiter was so impressed that he drank the Bronx straight down – in one go. Many bartenders now claim that the Bronx is the original juice-mixed cocktail.

077 **Bronx**
2 oz / 56 ml gin
¾ oz / 21 ml dry vermouth
¾ oz / 21 ml sweet vermouth
1 ½ oz / 42 ml orange juice

GLASS TYPE: ▢
ALCOHOL RATING: ●●●◐○
STAR RATING: ★★★★☆

Shake all of the ingredients together with ice and strain into an ice-filled glass. Drop in a cherry to garnish.

078▲ **cowboy 45**

2 mint leaves
1 oz / 28 ml gin
½ oz lemon juice
½ tsp powdered (caster) sugar
champagne

GLASS TYPE:
ALCOHOL RATING: ●●○○○
STAR RATING: ★★★☆☆

Muddle the mint leaves in a shaker. Add the gin, lemon and sugar. Shake with ice and strain into the glass. Top with champagne.

If you prefer your cocktail free of mint pieces, then you can strain the mix through a tea strainer.

079 **polo cocktail**

2 oz / 56 ml gin
1 tbsp lemon juice
1 tbsp orange juice

GLASS TYPE:
ALCOHOL RATING: ●●○○○
STAR RATING: ★★☆☆☆

Shake the ingredients together with ice and strain into the glass.

This cocktail is an acquired taste – the small measures of lemon and orange add a slight sourness to the flavour of the gin.

080 crimson cocktail

2 oz / 56 ml gin
1 oz / 28 ml port (sweet)
juice of ½ lemon
1 tsp grenadine

GLASS TYPE: ☐
ALCOHOL RATING: ●●●○○
STAR RATING: ★★★★☆

Shake all the ingredients together with ice and strain into an ice-filled glass. Put a mint leaf inside the glass to garnish.

The port gives this after-dinner cocktail a sweet and strongly alcoholic flavour.

081 morro

1 oz / 28 ml gin
½ oz / 14 ml dark rum
1 tbsp lime juice
1 tbsp pineapple juice
½ tsp powdered (caster) sugar

GLASS TYPE: ☐
ALCOHOL RATING: ●●○○○
STAR RATING: ★★★★★

Shake all the ingredients together with ice and strain into a sugar-rimmed old-fashioned glass filled with ice.

Leave this drink to stand for a few minutes before you start to drink it – this will help to bring out all its flavours.

082 Jamaica glow

1 oz / 28 ml gin
1 tbsp Claret
1 tsp Jamaica dark rum
1 tbsp orange juice

GLASS TYPE: ♈
ALCOHOL RATING: ●●○○○
STAR RATING: ★★★★☆

Shake all the ingredients together with ice and strain into the glass.

I think this cocktail works best with a full-bodied, fruity Claret as it complements the rum, but you can try it with any good red wine.

083 knock-out

¾ oz / 21 ml gin
¾ oz / 21 ml dry vermouth
½ oz / 14 ml anise-infused vodka
1 tsp crème de menthe (white)

GLASS TYPE: ♈
ALCOHOL RATING: ●●●●○
STAR RATING: ★★★★☆

Pour all the ingredients into a shaker, stir with ice and strain into the glass. Drop in a cherry to garnish.

To infuse your own vodka see p.21. Alternatively, you can use the liquorice-flavoured liqueur sambuca (see no.323) in place of the anise-infused vodka. Beware – this cocktail definitely lives up to its name.

about the bramble

The Bramble is a truly modern classic. Not only does it capture the essence of the time and place in which it was created, but it has gone on to enjoy international fame and popularity as well. Invented in the mid-1980s by legendary British bartender Dick Bradsell at Fred's Bar in London's Soho, the Bramble is a drink that defined a generation. The cocktail helped to usher in a new, prosperous era in London which saw a resurgence in cocktail bars and cocktail-drinking, and provided inspiration in its innovative blend of new liqueurs with traditional mixing methods. This is a fruity, heady drink that strikes the perfect balance between sweet and sour with an added blackberry tang. Variations on the Bramble can be made with almost any fruit liqueur in the place of blackberry, such as raspberry, strawberry, orange or apricot.

084   **bramble**

2 oz / 56 ml gin
juice of ½ lemon
½ oz / 14 ml sugar syrup
½ oz / 14 ml crème de mûre

GLASS TYPE: ▢
ALCOHOL RATING: ●●○○○
STAR RATING: ★★★★☆

Fill the glass with crushed ice. Pour in the first 3 ingredients. Stir. If necessary, add more crushed ice to fill the glass, and lace the drink with the crème de mûre. Garnish with 2 blackberries (pictured), and a lemon slice if desired.

085

gin Alexander

1 oz / 28 ml gin
1 oz / 28 ml crème de cacao (white)
1 oz / 28 ml single cream

GLASS TYPE: ♈
ALCOHOL RATING: ●●◖○○
STAR RATING: ★★☆☆☆

Shake the ingredients together with ice and strain into the glass.
To garnish, sprinkle nutmeg on the top of the drink.
Believe it or not the garnish is the most flavoursome ingredient in this cocktail.
You may want to add a dash of sugar syrup to sweeten.

086

Harlem

1 ½ oz / 42 ml gin
½ tsp maraschino
¾ oz / 21 ml pineapple juice

GLASS TYPE: ♈
ALCOHOL RATING: ●◖○○○
STAR RATING: ★★★★★

Shake the ingredients with ice and strain into the glass. Put a pineapple
slice, or wedge, on the rim of the glass to decorate.
Using maraschino is a good way of mixing gin with other juices, as the maraschino
enhances the flavour of the fruit juice.

087

Belmont

2 oz / 56 ml gin
¾ oz / 21 ml single cream
1 tsp raspberry purée

GLASS TYPE: ♈
ALCOHOL RATING: ●●◖○○
STAR RATING: ★★☆☆☆

Shake the ingredients together with ice and strain into the glass. Drop
2 fresh raspberries into the drink to garnish.
Delicious – raspberries and cream. You can use frozen purée – however, the drink
will taste fresher and much better if you make the purée yourself (see pp. 16–17).

088

jockey club

1 ½ oz / 42 ml gin
¼ tsp crème de cacao (white)
dash Angostura bitters
juice of ¼ lemon

GLASS TYPE: ♈
ALCOHOL RATING: ●◖○○○
STAR RATING: ★★★★☆

Shake all the ingredients together with ice and strain into the glass.
Cacao and lemon may seem a surprising combination, but they complement each
other in this gin mix. The different flavours hit the taste buds separately – first the
chocolate, then the gin, finished with a lemon aftertaste.

089▲ **Singapore sling**
2 oz / 56 ml gin
juice of ½ lemon
1 tsp powdered (caster) sugar
soda
½ oz / 14 ml cherry brandy

GLASS TYPE: 🍺 🍺
ALCOHOL RATING: ●●◐○○
STAR RATING: ★★★★☆

Pour the gin, lemon and sugar into a glass filled with ice. Stir. Add the soda, leaving just enough room to float the cherry brandy on top. To garnish, place a lemon wheel inside the glass, and drop in a cherry if desired.
This cocktail was invented by Ngiam Tong Boon, a bartender at the Long Bar in Singapore's Raffles Hotel, around 1915. A first-rate drink, and if I were a big gin drinker this would be the cocktail for me. The drink can be served in a pilsner or a highball glass.

090

gin sling

2 oz / 56 ml gin
juice of ½ lemon
1 tsp powdered (caster) sugar
soda

GLASS TYPE: ⬜
ALCOHOL RATING: ●●◔○○
STAR RATING: ★★★☆☆

Pour the gin, lemon and sugar into a glass filled with ice. Stir until the sugar has dissolved. Top with soda. Stir again. Drop in an orange twist to garnish.
Singapore Sling? No, Gin Sling. Why? Well, it's minus the cherry brandy, which turns it into a sharper-tasting and opaque-looking drink.

091▼

orange oasis

1 ½ oz / 42 ml gin
½ oz / 14 ml kirsch
4 oz / 112 ml orange juice
ginger ale

GLASS TYPE: ⬜
ALCOHOL RATING: ●●○○○
STAR RATING: ★★★★☆

Shake the first 3 ingredients with ice and strain into an ice-filled glass. Top with ginger ale and stir. Garnish with an orange slice.
This refreshing summer cocktail tastes like fizzy orange with a hint of bitter cherry.

COCKTAILS 089 TO 091

092 Palm Beach

1 ½ oz / 42 ml gin
1 ½ tsp sweet vermouth
1 ½ tsp grapefruit juice

GLASS TYPE: Y
ALCOHOL RATING: ●●●○○
STAR RATING: ★★★★☆

Shake the ingredients together with ice and strain into the glass.
Not for the sweet-toothed – although this mix contains sweet vermouth, it's a very dry and bitter cocktail.

093 tuxedo

1 ½ oz / 42 ml gin
1 ½ oz / 42 ml dry vermouth
¼ tsp Pernod
¼ tsp maraschino
2 dashes orange bitters

GLASS TYPE: Y
ALCOHOL RATING: ●●●●○
STAR RATING: ★★★★★

Pour all of the ingredients into a shaker, stir with ice and strain the mix into the glass. Drop a cherry into the glass to garnish.
This cocktail also tastes good with a champagne top.

094 kiss-in-the-dark

¾ oz / 21 ml gin
¾ oz / 21 ml cherry brandy
¾ oz / 21 ml dry vermouth

GLASS TYPE: Y
ALCOHOL RATING: ●●○○○
STAR RATING: ★★★☆☆

Pour the ingredients into a shaker, stir with ice and strain into the glass.
This subtle blend of gin and cherry creates a pleasant, dry mix.

095 gin Rickey

1 ½ oz / 42 ml gin
juice of ½ lime
soda

GLASS TYPE: ▯
ALCOHOL RATING: ●○○○○
STAR RATING: ★★★☆☆

Pour the gin and the lime juice into a glass filled with ice. Fill with soda. Stir. Put a lime wedge into the drink to garnish.
Although a rickey can be made with brandy, whiskey or rum (it must include the sourness of lime or lemon juice, and soda), the Gin Rickey is the original drink. First made at Shoemaker's Restaurant in Washington for a congressional lobbyist named Joe Rickey, the cocktail dates from the late 19th century. You may wish to add a dash of sugar syrup to sweeten.

096 **merry widow**

1 ¼ oz / 35 ml gin
1 ¼ oz / 35 ml dry vermouth
½ tsp Bénédictine
½ tsp Pernod
dash orange bitters

GLASS TYPE: Y
ALCOHOL RATING: ●●●○○
STAR RATING: ★★★☆☆

Pour all of the ingredients into a shaker, stir with ice and strain into the glass. Place a lemon peel into the drink to garnish.

Instead of using Pernod you can try infusing your own gin with anise (see p.21) to enhance the herb and liquorice flavours of this drink.

097 **abbey cocktail**

1 ½ oz / 42 ml gin
dash orange bitters
juice of ¼ orange

GLASS TYPE: Y
ALCOHOL RATING: ●◑○○○
STAR RATING: ★★☆☆☆

Shake the ingredients with ice and strain into the glass. Put a cherry inside the glass to garnish.

This drink really needs the bitters to give it that extra orange zest.

098 **crystal slipper**

1 ½ oz / 42 ml gin
½ oz / 14 ml blue curaçao
2 dashes orange bitters

GLASS TYPE: Y
ALCOHOL RATING: ●●○○○
STAR RATING: ★★★☆☆

Pour the ingredients into a shaker, shake with ice and strain into the glass. Place an orange twist inside the glass to garnish.

A blue, orange-flavoured gin martini – quaint but simple.

099 **Honolulu no. 1**

1 ½ oz / 42 ml gin
dash Angostura bitters
dash lemon juice
dash orange juice
dash pineapple juice
½ tsp powdered (caster) sugar

GLASS TYPE: Y
ALCOHOL RATING: ●◑○○○
STAR RATING: ★★★★☆

Pour all the ingredients into a shaker, shake with ice and strain the mix into the glass.

This mix of juice and bitters creates a refreshing blend with herbal undertones.

tequila

Tequila, the base of America's number-one cocktail, the Margarita (see no.119), is regarded as North America's first ever commercially-produced spirit. The drink hails from the town of Tequila in the heart of Mexico and is made from the distilled sap of the blue agave plant which is native to the high plains of Jalisco state. Tequila, which can be clear or golden in colour, must contain a minimum of 51% agave to earn its name, and can be found to contain up to 100% agave. The higher the agave content, the better (and more expensive) the tequila.

Agave plants may have been used to make a forerunner to tequila as long ago as the 13th century. Archaeologists believe that the Aztecs brewed an agave-based drink (pulque) for ceremonial and ritual use (brutal penalties were in place for those who consumed the drink for pleasure alone!). Then, when the 16th-century Spanish conquistadors arrived in Mexico, they brought with them distillation techniques and began distilling, rather than simply fermenting, pulque to make a drink much closer to the tequila we know today. In the 1700s Tequilan entrepreneur, José Cuervo, first bottled the distilled liquor for sale.

100 wild thing

1 ½ oz / 42 ml tequila
1 oz / 28 ml cranberry juice
½ oz / 14 ml lime juice
1 oz / 28 ml soda

GLASS TYPE: ▯
ALCOHOL RATING: ●◐○○○
STAR RATING: ★★★★☆

Pour the first 3 ingredients into a glass filled with ice. Top with soda.
To garnish, put a lime wheel inside the glass.
This smooth and refreshing cocktail goes down really easily and quickly.

101 purple poncho

1 oz / 28 ml tequila
½ oz / 14 ml blue curaçao
½ oz / 14 ml sloe gin
juice of 1 lime
dash sugar syrup

GLASS TYPE: ▽
ALCOHOL RATING: ●●○○○
STAR RATING: ★★★☆☆

Pour all of the ingredients into a shaker, shake with ice and strain the mix
into the glass. Place a lime wheel on the rim of the glass to decorate.
The mix of curaçao and sloe gin creates a sweet, herbal-flavoured cocktail.

102 tequila canyon

1 ½ oz / 42 ml tequila
dash triple sec
4 oz / 112 ml cranberry juice
¼ oz / 7 ml orange juice
¼ oz / 7 ml pineapple juice

GLASS TYPE: ▯
ALCOHOL RATING: ●◐○○○
STAR RATING: ★★★★☆

Pour all of the ingredients into a glass filled with ice. Stir gently. Put a lime
wheel inside the glass to garnish.
The sweetness of the pineapple takes the edge off the bitter cranberry,
and the whole fruit taste balances the tequila – a great summer drink.

103 south of the border

1 oz / 28 ml tequila
¾ oz / 21 ml Kalúha
juice of ½ lime

GLASS TYPE: ▯
ALCOHOL RATING: ●◐○○○
STAR RATING: ★★★★☆

Shake all the ingredients together with ice and strain into an ice-filled glass.
Place a slice of lime inside the glass to garnish.
The lime will bring out the sourness of the tequila, while the combination
of the Kalúha and tequila will create a rich flavour to tantalize your taste buds at
the end of each sip.

104 tequila pink

1 ½ oz / 42 ml tequila
1 oz / 28 ml dry vermouth
dash grenadine

GLASS TYPE: 𝖸
ALCOHOL RATING: ●●◑○○
STAR RATING: ★★★☆☆

Shake the ingredients together with ice and strain into the glass.
Although the grenadine adds sweetness to this cocktail, it is still a strong,
tequila-flavoured drink.

105▼ catalina margarita

1 ½ oz / 42 ml tequila
1 oz / 28 ml blue curaçao
1 oz / 28 ml peach schnapps
4 oz / 112 ml sour mix (see p.17)

GLASS TYPE: 𝖸
ALCOHOL RATING: ●●●◑○
STAR RATING: ★★★★★

Shake all the ingredients with ice and strain into a chilled margarita glass.
Garnish with a lime twist.
The chilled glass will help to keep this slow-sipping drink cool right to the last taste.

tequila sunrise

2 oz / 56 ml tequila
4 oz / 112 ml orange juice
¾ oz / 21 ml grenadine

GLASS TYPE:
ALCOHOL RATING: ●●○○○
STAR RATING: ★★★★☆

Pour the tequila and the orange into a shaker, stir with ice and strain into a glass. Add ice cubes. Pour in the grenadine and allow it to sink down to the bottom of the drink to complete your sunrise. Garnish with a lime wheel. If desired, serve this drink with a straw, so that the grenadine will be the first flavour to hit the palate, and the stronger-tasting tequila will be disguised right to the end of the drink.

MODERN CLASSIC

about the tequila sunrise

A hugely popular, easy-drinking modern classic, the Tequila Sunrise evokes images of palm-fringed beaches and balmy evenings in exotic locations. This is a fruity and refreshing cocktail with a powerful tequila kick that is effortlessly masked by the sweet-tasting grenadine. The grenadine is always added last so that it streaks red through the orange drink as it slowly sinks to the bottom of the glass to give the famous "sunrise" effect.

Although its image has suffered a little in recent years from a backlash against the genre of colourful and elaborately-garnished fruit cocktails, the Tequila Sunrise remains a popular classic — easy to mix and even easier to drink, it is a great introduction to the cocktail world.

107 **hairy sunrise**

¾ oz / 21 ml tequila
¾ oz / 21 ml vodka
½ oz / 14 ml triple sec
3 oz / 84 ml orange juice
2 or 3 dashes grenadine

GLASS TYPE:
ALCOHOL RATING: ●◑○○○
STAR RATING: ★★★☆☆

Blend the first four ingredients together with a cup of ice until the mixture is smooth. Pour the mix into a glass. Carefully pour in the grenadine. Put a slice of lime and a sprig of mint inside the glass to garnish.
Blending the ingredients will dilute this mix. The grenadine will trickle down into the drink, giving the appearance of hair – hence this cocktail's name.

108 **Mexicana**

1 ½ oz / 42 ml tequila
1 oz / 28 ml lemon juice
1 tbsp pineapple juice
1 tsp grenadine

GLASS TYPE: ▽
ALCOHOL RATING: ●◑○○○
STAR RATING: ★★★☆☆

Shake all the ingredients together with ice and strain into the glass. Put a lime wheel and a pineapple leaf inside the glass to garnish.
The grenadine enhances the sweetness of the pineapple. The lemon adds a hint of sourness. In essence, this is an easy-to-drink, sweet and sour cocktail.

109 **Tijuana taxi**

2 oz / 56 ml gold tequila
1 oz / 28 ml blue curaçao
1 oz / 20 ml liqueur of choice
soda

GLASS TYPE:
ALCOHOL RATING: ●●●◑○
STAR RATING: ★★★☆☆

Pour the tequila, curaçao and liqueur into a glass filled with ice. Fill with soda. Drop in a cherry to garnish.
The liqueur is needed to sweeten this otherwise strong-tasting cocktail. Personally, I like to use crème de framboises or parfait amour.

110 **shady lady**

1 oz / 28 ml tequila
1 oz / 28 ml Midori
4 oz / 112 ml grapefruit juice

GLASS TYPE:
ALCOHOL RATING: ●●○○○
STAR RATING: ★★★★★

Pour the ingredients into a glass filled with ice. Put a lime wheel and a cherry into the drink to garnish.
For a more fruity flavour add a large slice of honeydew melon: muddle the fruit in a shaker, then add the listed ingredients; shake and strain into an ice-filled glass.

111 tequila old-fashioned

1 orange peel
½ tsp sugar (brown)
dash Angostura bitters
1 ¾ oz / 49 ml tequila
soda

GLASS TYPE: ⬚
ALCOHOL RATING: ●◑○○○
STAR RATING: ★★★★☆

Mix the orange peel together with the sugar, bitters and a dash of tequila in an old-fashioned glass. Pour in the remaining tequila. While stirring, slowly add ice to chill the glass. Top with soda and place a pineapple stick inside the glass to garnish.

The pineapple will release enough flavour to ensure that the drink isn't too bitter, and the water will help to temper the taste so that the mix can be drunk straight away.

112 la bomba

1 ½ oz / 42 ml gold tequila
¾ oz / 21 ml triple sec
2 dashes apricot brandy
1 ½ oz / 42 ml orange juice
1 ½ oz / 42 ml pineapple juice

GLASS TYPE: ▽
ALCOHOL RATING: ●●○○○
STAR RATING: ★★★☆☆

Shake all the ingredients together with ice and pour into a sugar-rimmed glass. Place a lime wheel on the rim of the glass to decorate.

For a healthier version, try this cocktail with freshly-muddled fruit. Simply muddle the fruit in a shaker, then add the alcohol; shake with ice and pour the mix into the glass. Garnish as before.

113 silk stockings

1 ½ oz / 42 ml tequila
1 oz / 28 ml crème de cacao (brown)
1 ½ oz / 42 ml single cream
dash grenadine

GLASS TYPE: ▽
ALCOHOL RATING: ●●○○○
STAR RATING: ★★★★☆

Shake all of the ingredients together with ice and strain into the glass. To garnish, sprinkle cinnamon on top, or put a cinnamon stick inside the glass.

A deliciously creamy after-dinner cocktail.

114 bulldog

1 ½ oz / 42 ml tequila
1 oz / 28 ml Kalúha

GLASS TYPE: ⬚
ALCOHOL RATING: ●●◑○○
STAR RATING: ★★★☆☆

Pour the ingredients into a glass filled with ice. Stir.
Place a twist of lemon inside the glass to garnish.

Kalúha is a sweet, coffee-flavoured liqueur, produced from Arabica coffee beans. This cocktail was invented in the late 20th century, in Mexico – the birthplace of Kalúha.

THE TEQUILA BASE

74

Mexican Madras

1 oz / 28 ml gold tequila
3 oz / 84 ml cranberry juice
½ oz / 14 ml orange juice
dash lime juice

GLASS TYPE: ⊖
ALCOHOL RATING: ●◐○○○
STAR RATING: ★★★★☆

Pour all of the ingredients into a shaker, shake together with ice and strain
into a glass. Place a slice of orange inside the glass to garnish.
This is the harsher-tasting tequila version of the vodka Madras (see no.26).

tequila collins

2 oz / 56 ml tequila
juice of ½ lemon
1 tsp powdered (caster) sugar
soda

GLASS TYPE: ☐
ALCOHOL RATING: ●●○○○
STAR RATING: ★★★★☆

Shake all the ingredients (except for the soda) with ice and strain into
an ice-filled glass. Top with soda and stir. To garnish, put a loose twist
of lemon and a loose twist of orange inside the glass, and drop in a cherry.
*This is the tequila version of the classic gin-based Tom Collins (see no.57). Often,
cocktails that contain fizzy drinks are not stirred. However, this mix should be stirred
to ensure that the sugar dissolves completely.*

crushing Hazel

1 oz / 28 ml tequila
dash crème de cacao (white)
dash Frangelico
dash single cream

GLASS TYPE: Y
ALCOHOL RATING: ●◐○○○
STAR RATING: ★★★★☆

Shake all the ingredients together with ice and strain into the glass. Sprinkle
with crushed hazelnuts to garnish.
*Frangelico is an Italian liqueur made from herbs, berries and hazelnuts. The liqueur
adds a sweet, nutty flavour to this great after-dinner cocktail.*

tequini

1 ½ oz / 42 ml tequila
½ oz / 14 ml dry vermouth
dash Angostura bitters (optional)

GLASS TYPE: Y
ALCOHOL RATING: ●●○○○
STAR RATING: ★★★★☆

Pour the ingredients into a shaker, stir with ice and strain into the glass.
To garnish, put a twist of lemon and an olive inside the glass.
*This is a martini made with tequila instead of vodka or gin. If you choose to include
the bitters in the mix, they will add a subtle, herbal note.*

about the Margarita

The Margarita is thought to have been first mixed in the 1940s (although some say the 1930s), and it remains one of the most popular cocktails in the US today – in particular, for making, serving and drinking at home.

For cocktail connoisseurs the origin of the Margarita is a hotly debated subject. One of the more consistently recounted stories tells of a flamboyant Dallas socialite named Margarita Samas. Margarita hosted incredible parties and loved to entertain her guests with exotic alcoholic mixes that she herself had conjured up. Offering the mixes to anyone brave enough to try, she would ask them first to guess the contents and then to pass judgment on the taste. At Christmas in 1948, at her vacation home in Acapulco (on the Pacific coast of Mexico), Margarita hosted a poolside party for her Texan friends and family. It was at this party that she produced a mix of tequila, triple sec and lime juice. Her guests loved it and the blend soon became the society drink of the southern US, spreading quickly (from Acapulco) through Texas to Hollywood. It was named, of course, the Margarita. An alternative story is that the Spaniard Enrique Bastante Gutiérrez, who was a world-champion cocktail mixer in the 1940s, was the first to mix the drink – he is said to have done so especially for screen icon Rita Heyworth. There is also the tale of Marjorie King, a showgirl who was allegedly allergic to all alcohol except for tequila. While visiting the Rancho Del Gloria Bar on Rosarita Beach, Mexico, in 1938, she requested a mixed drink rather than a regular shot. The bartender, Danny Herrera, poured tequila over shaved ice, adding lime and triple sec. He translated Marjorie's name into Spanish, thus creating the Margarita.

119 **Margarita**
2 oz / 56 ml gold tequila
1 oz / 28 ml triple sec
juice of ½ lime

GLASS TYPE: 🍸
ALCOHOL RATING: ●●●○○
STAR RATING: ★★★★★

Shake all the ingredients together with ice and strain into a chilled, salt-rimmed glass. To garnish cut a thin slice of fresh lime and halve it. Place one half inside the glass and the other on the rim.

sloe tequila

1 oz / 28 ml tequila
½ oz / 14 ml sloe gin
1 tbsp lime juice

GLASS TYPE: ▽
ALCOHOL RATING: ●◐○○○
STAR RATING: ★★★★★

Blend the ingredients together with half a cup of ice and pour into the glass.
Add 3 ice cubes. Put a twisted cucumber peel inside the glass to garnish.
This is a wonderfully smooth and fresh-tasting combination.

121▼ ## strawberry margarita

3 strawberries
1 oz / 28 ml tequila
½ oz / 14 ml strawberry liqueur
½ oz / 14 ml triple sec
juice of ½ lime

GLASS TYPE: ▽
ALCOHOL RATING: ●●○○○
STAR RATING: ★★★★★

Muddle the strawberries in a shaker. Add the remaining ingredients. Shake
with ice and strain into a sugar-rimmed glass. Float 2 strawberry slices on top.
*You can substitute the strawberry with other fresh fruit – try raspberry, kiwi or
mango. Be sure to sugar-rim the glass to complement the sweetness of the fruit.*

122▲ pom-amore

¼ pomegranate
dash sugar syrup
1 ½ oz / 42 ml tequila
¼ oz / 7 ml parfait amour

Squeeze the pomegranate into the shaker to release the flesh. Muddle the flesh with the sugar. Add the tequila and parfait amour. Shake with ice and strain into the glass. To garnish, drop in 10 to 15 pips from the remaining half of the pomegranate, and float a pansy head on top of the drink.

This is one of my favourite cocktails that I have ever created – the ingredients mix so well. You can garnish your own drink with any edible flower that you desire.

123 tequila manhattan

2 oz / 56 ml tequila
1 oz / 28 ml sweet vermouth
dash lime juice

Shake the ingredients with ice and strain the mix into a glass containing 1 ice cube. Drop a cherry and an orange peel into the drink to garnish.

This is a refined drink for serious tequila lovers.

124   **traffic light cooler**

¾ oz / 21 ml Midori
1 oz / 28 ml gold tequila
splash sour mix (see p.17)
2 oz / 56 ml orange juice
½ oz / 14 ml sloe gin

GLASS TYPE: ⊓
ALCOHOL RATING: ●●◔○○
STAR RATING: ★★★☆☆

To layer this drink: first pour the Midori into a pilsner glass filled with ice.
Then add the tequila, to create a layer of green. Pour in the sour mix.
Slowly add the orange juice, pouring against the side of the glass, to create
an amber layer. Carefully float the sloe gin on top for the red layer. Place a
lemon wheel, a lime wheel and a cherry inside the glass to garnish.
*To preserve the 3 colourful layers of this cocktail serve unstirred – but provide
a swizzle stick, so that the drinker can mix at their leisure.*

125   **Pacific sunshine**

1 ½ oz / 42 ml tequila
1 ½ oz / 42 ml blue curaçao
1 ½ oz / 42 ml sour mix (see p.17)
dash Angostura bitters

GLASS TYPE: ⊓
ALCOHOL RATING: ●●●○○
STAR RATING: ★★★☆☆

Stir all the ingredients together with ice and pour into a chilled,
salted-rimmed glass. Put a lemon wheel inside the glass to garnish.
The bitters add a herbal flavour to this sour drink.

126   **blue margarita**

1 ½ oz / 42 ml tequila
½ oz / 14 ml blue curaçao
1 oz / 28 ml lime juice

GLASS TYPE: ▽
ALCOHOL RATING: ●●○○○
STAR RATING: ★★★☆☆

Shake the ingredients together with ice and strain into a salt-rimmed glass.
Place a loose orange twist inside the glass to garnish.
*Alternatively, try blending the ingredients together with a cup of ice. This will give
the drink an opaque-blue appearance.*

127   **tequila mockingbird**

1 ½ oz / 42 ml tequila
¾ oz / 21 ml crème de menthe (green)
juice of 1 lime

GLASS TYPE: ▽
ALCOHOL RATING: ●●◔○○
STAR RATING: ★★☆☆☆

Shake all the ingredients together with ice and strain into the glass.
*If, like me, you aren't a fan of crème de menthe, you can use fresh mint and a dash
of sugar syrup: simply muddle the mint in a shaker, then add the tequila, lime and
sugar. Shake with ice and strain the mix into the glass.*

128 chapala

1 ½ oz / 42 ml tequila
1 tsp apricot brandy
1 tsp blue curaçao
dash triple sec
1 tbsp lemon juice
1 tbsp orange juice

GLASS TYPE: ▯
ALCOHOL RATING: ●◑○○○
STAR RATING: ★★★☆☆

Pour all the ingredients into a shaker, shake with ice and strain into an ice-filled glass. Put a slice of orange inside the glass to garnish.
If drunk slowly this is a refreshing cocktail, and it is a good apéritif – for food or another drink!

129 tequila sour

2 oz / 56 ml tequila
juice of ½ lemon
1 tsp powdered (caster) sugar
dash egg white (optional)

GLASS TYPE: ▯
ALCOHOL RATING: ●●○○○
STAR RATING: ★★★★★

Shake the ingredients with ice and strain into the glass. Put a slice of lemon and a cherry inside the glass to garnish.
If shaken with egg white (see p.16), this drink will have a frothy, cappuccino-like head. The egg white will have only a slight impact on the flavour.

130 hot pants

1 ½ oz / 42 ml tequila
¼ oz / 14 ml liqueur of choice
1 tbsp grapefruit juice
2 mint leaves
1 tsp powdered (caster) sugar

GLASS TYPE: ▯
ALCOHOL RATING: ●●○○○
STAR RATING: ★★★☆☆

Shake all the ingredients together with ice and pour into an ice-filled glass. Put a sprig of mint on top of the ice to garnish.
This drink works well with any flavour liqueur. Peach is my personal favourite.

131 Rosita

1 oz / 28 ml tequila
1 oz / 28 ml Campari
½ oz / 14 ml dry vermouth
½ oz / 14 ml sweet vermouth

GLASS TYPE: ▯
ALCOHOL RATING: ●●◑○○
STAR RATING: ★★★★☆

Pour the ingredients into an ice-filled glass and stir. Place a lemon peel inside the glass to garnish.
The combination of the 3 types of vermouth make this cocktail an excellent apéritif.

132 cactus berry

1 ¼ oz / 35 ml tequila
1 ¼ oz / 35 ml red wine
1 oz / 28 ml triple sec
6 ½ oz / 182 ml sour mix (see p.17)
dash lime juice

GLASS TYPE: ⍋
ALCOHOL RATING: ●●●◍○
STAR RATING: ★★★☆☆

Shake all of the ingredients with ice and pour into a salt-rimmed glass.
*This is a good party cocktail. The red wine turns this drink into a sangria-tasting
margarita. I find that oaky-flavoured wines work well with tequila. You may wish
to add a splash of soda to temper the alcohol.*

133 mexicola

2 oz / 56 ml tequila
juice of ½ lime
cola

GLASS TYPE: ▯
ALCOHOL RATING: ●●○○○
STAR RATING: ★★★☆☆

Pour the tequila and the lime juice into a glass filled with ice. Fill with cola
and stir. Drop in a lime wedge to garnish.
*If you are ordering this drink in a bar ask for cola from a bottle, as the cola usually
served on tap is too sweet for this drink. If you have no option, ask for more lime
to counterbalance the sweetness.*

134 teutonic

2 oz / 56 ml tequila
juice of 1 lime or ½ lemon
tonic water

GLASS TYPE: ▢
ALCOHOL RATING: ●●○○○
STAR RATING: ★★★☆☆

Pour the first 2 ingredients into a glass filled with ice. Top with tonic water
and stir. Put a slice of lemon and a slice of lime inside the glass to garnish.
*The juice of the lemon or lime will temper this biting mix of tequila and tonic,
to create a refreshing cocktail.*

135 tequila matador

1 ½ oz / 42 ml tequila
3 oz / 84 ml pineapple juice
juice of ½ lime

GLASS TYPE: ▢ ⍋
ALCOHOL RATING: ●●○○○
STAR RATING: ★★★★☆

Shake the ingredients together with ice and strain into an ice-filled
old-fashioned glass. Put a pineapple leaf inside the glass to garnish.
*Try this cocktail with a dash of champagne: simply shake the ingredients with
ice and strain the mix into a flute. Top with champagne and garnish as before.*

136 toreador

1 ½ oz / 42 ml tequila
½ oz / 14 ml crème de cacao (brown)
1 tbsp single cream

GLASS TYPE: ♉
ALCOHOL RATING: ●●○○○
STAR RATING: ★★★☆☆

Shake the ingredients with ice and strain into the glass. Garnish with
a sprinkle of cocoa powder.

This is a satisfying after dinner cocktail.

137▾ purple gecko

1 ½ oz / 42 ml tequila
½ oz / 14 ml blue curaçao
1 ½ oz / 42 ml cranberry juice
1 oz / 28 ml sour mix (see p.17)
½ oz / 14 ml lime juice

GLASS TYPE: ♉ ♉
ALCOHOL RATING: ●●○○○
STAR RATING: ★★★★☆

Shake all of the ingredients together with ice and strain into a salt-rimmed
glass. Garnish with a lime wedge.

The cranberry gives this version of a margarita a distinctive "berry" taste.

rum

Rum originated in the West Indies some two hundred years after Columbus first introduced sugar cane there in the 15th century. Today, rum can be made wherever the crop grows (including South America, South Africa, India and Australia), but its main centre of production remains the islands of the Caribbean.

Rum is made from either distilled sugar-cane juice or fermented molasses, and is aged in oak casks. The spirit can be divided into two main categories: light and dark. Light rum is ready to drink in less than a year and is usually clear and light in taste and body. Dark rum (which gains its colour through the addition of caramel) is aged from 3 to 12 years and is heavy-bodied with a deep, rich flavour. A third type, gold rum, falls between the two: its colour is gained through a short maturation in the oak casks (sometimes caramel is added).

Puerto Rico, Cuba and Barbados are the main producers of light rum and Jamaica, Guyana and Haiti the best-known producers of dark rum. Havana Club is the best brand of gold rum. Brazil makes its own type of rum, known as cachaça (see the classic Caipirinha, no.174).

138   Caribbean romance

1 ½ oz / 42 ml light rum
1 oz / 28 ml amaretto
1 ½ oz / 42 ml orange juice
1 ½ oz / 42 ml pineapple juice
splash grenadine

GLASS TYPE: 🥃
ALCOHOL RATING: ●●○○○
STAR RATING: ★★★☆☆

Pour the first 4 ingredients into a shaker, shake with ice and strain into
an ice-filled glass. Add the grenadine. To garnish, place a slice of orange,
lemon or lime on the rim of the glass.
The combination of almond and rum sets a romantic tone for this cocktail.

139   quarter deck

1 ½ oz / 42 ml light rum
¼ oz / 7 ml sherry
juice of ½ lime

GLASS TYPE: 🍸
ALCOHOL RATING: ●●○○○
STAR RATING: ★★★★☆

Pour the ingredients into a shaker. Stir with ice and strain into the glass.
The sherry gives this cocktail a creamy taste.

140   Boston cooler

juice of ½ lemon
1 tsp powdered (caster) sugar
4 oz / 112 ml ginger ale or soda
2 oz / 56 ml light rum

GLASS TYPE: 🥃
ALCOHOL RATING: ●●○○○
STAR RATING: ★★★☆☆

Pour the lemon juice, sugar and 2 oz/56 ml of ginger ale or soda into
the glass and stir. Fill the glass with ice, then add the rum. Top with the
remaining ginger ale or soda and stir again. To garnish, put a slice of lemon
inside the glass.
*A light and simple drink to serve at parties – everyone will love it. As an alternative,
you can make this drink with 2 oz/56 ml of ginger ale and 2 oz/56 ml of soda.*

141   knickerbocker special

2 oz / 56 ml light rum
½ tsp triple sec
1 tsp lemon juice
1 tsp orange juice
1 tsp raspberry syrup

GLASS TYPE: 🍸
ALCOHOL RATING: ●●○○○
STAR RATING: ★★★★☆

Shake all the ingredients together with ice and strain into the glass. Place
2 raspberries and an orange slice inside the glass to garnish.
This is quite a strong, slightly zesty-tasting drink.

142 rum fix

juice of 1 lime or ½ lemon
1 tsp water (warm)
1 tsp powdered (caster) sugar
2 ½ oz / 70 ml light rum

GLASS TYPE: ▢
ALCOHOL RATING: ●●◑○○
STAR RATING: ★★★★★

Pour the first 3 ingredients into a glass and stir. Fill the glass with ice. Pour in the rum and stir again. Put a slice of lemon inside the glass to garnish.
A fix is any short, strong, spirit-based cocktail served with ice in an old-fashioned glass. Stir the ingredients together with fresh mint to make a Rum Smash.

143 Nevada

1 ½ oz / 42 ml light rum
dash Angostura bitters
juice of 1 lime
1 oz / 28 ml grapefruit juice
3 tsp powdered (caster) sugar

GLASS TYPE: Y
ALCOHOL RATING: ●◑○○○
STAR RATING: ★★★★☆

Shake all of the ingredients together with ice and strain into the glass.
This is a sour-tasting cocktail with bitter undertones.

144 apple pie no. 1

1 oz / 28 ml light rum
½ oz / 14 ml sweet vermouth
1 tbsp apple schnapps
1 tsp lemon juice
½ tsp grenadine

GLASS TYPE: Y
ALCOHOL RATING: ●●○○○
STAR RATING: ★★★☆☆

Shake all the ingredients together with ice and strain into the glass.
To garnish, place 3 thinly sliced pieces of apple inside the glass.
Apple pie? What kind of name is that for a cocktail? Once you taste it you'll be in no doubt as to how it got its name. The blend is a good appetite stabilizer, and so is usually drunk as an apéritif.

145 Tahiti club

2 oz / 56 ml light rum
½ tsp maraschino
1 oz / 28 ml pineapple juice
1 tbsp lemon juice
1 tbsp lime juice

GLASS TYPE: ▢
ALCOHOL RATING: ●●○○○
STAR RATING: ★★★☆☆

Shake all the ingredients together with ice and strain into an ice-filled glass.
Drop in a slice of lemon to garnish.
This cocktail is a complementary mix of sharp and sweet flavours – a great early-evening drink.

Shanghai Noon

146

1 oz / 28 ml Jamaica light rum
1 tsp Pernod
juice of ¼ lemon
½ tsp grenadine

GLASS TYPE: ▽
ALCOHOL RATING: ●◐○○○
STAR RATING: ★★★★★

Shake all the ingredients together with ice and strain into the glass. Place
a lemon peel inside the glass to garnish.
The Pernod adds an anise aroma and flavour to the caramel-tasting Jamaican rum.
Remember the 2000 movie Shanghai Noon starring action hero Jackie Chan? Well,
drink too many of these and the next morning you'll be hanging!

cool blue

147

1 ½ oz / 42 ml dark rum
2 oz / 56 ml cranberry juice
2 oz / 56 ml pineapple juice
splash sour mix (see p.17)
1 oz / 28 ml blue curaçao

GLASS TYPE: ▯
ALCOHOL RATING: ●●◐○○
STAR RATING: ★★★☆☆

Shake all of the ingredients (except for the curaçao) together with ice,
and pour into an ice-filled glass. Float the curaçao on top. To garnish,
drop 2 slices of pineapple, 2 slices of orange and a cherry into the drink.
The sour cranberry and sweet pineapple complement each other in this
refreshing, blue-topped drink.

raspberry delight

148

6 fresh raspberries (plus 2 or 3 for garnish)
1 ½ oz / 42 ml light rum
½ tsp triple sec
1 tsp lemon juice
1 tsp orange juice
1 tsp raspberry purée

GLASS TYPE: ▽
ALCOHOL RATING: ●●◐○○
STAR RATING: ★★★★★

Muddle the fruit in a shaker. Pour in the remaining ingredients; shake
vigorously with ice and strain the mix into the glass. Put 2 or 3 raspberries
on the top to garnish.
A truly exceptional fresh-fruit cocktail – it's also great with fresh strawberries.

Cuban special

149

1 oz / 28 ml light rum
½ tsp triple sec
juice of ½ lime
1 tbsp pineapple juice

GLASS TYPE: ▽
ALCOHOL RATING: ●○○○○
STAR RATING: ★★★★☆

Shake all the ingredients together with ice and strain into the glass.
I usually leave this drink ungarnished, but if you want to decorate it, you can slip
in a slice of pineapple.

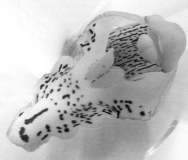

Mai Tai

1 oz / 28 ml dark rum
1 oz / 28 ml gold rum
1 oz / 28 ml triple sec
dash apricot brandy
2 oz / 56 ml pineapple juice
1 tbsp lime juice
1 tbsp orgeat syrup
splash orange juice
½ tsp powdered (caster) sugar

GLASS TYPE: ⧠
ALCOHOL RATING: ●●●◐○
STAR RATING: ★★★★★

Shake all the ingredients together with ice and strain into a glass one-third filled with crushed ice. Decorate with a cherry speared to a wedge of pineapple. Alternatively, for a true Polynesian effect, float an orchid on the top as shown. For a hair-raiser, top with a dash of 151-proof rum.

TRADITIONAL CLASSIC

about Mai Tai

A universally popular, exotic, fruity cocktail, the Mai Tai embodies that idyllic island feeling of white, sandy beaches with palm trees and fabulous sunsets. The drink originated on the west coast of the US, at the end of World War II, and its name and ingredients epitomized the kitsch version of Polynesian culture that US servicemen brought back with them from the South Pacific. The more fruit, umbrellas, Hawaiian shirts and garlands adorning the Mai Tai and its drinker, the better!

Today we are a little more restrained in our choice of garnishes, but this delicious, sweet cocktail remains a firm favourite with its kaleidoscope of tropical flavours which blend together perfectly – a true island delight.

151▲ **Daiquiri**
2 oz / 56 ml light rum
juice of 1 lime
1 tsp powdered (caster) sugar

GLASS TYPE: ϓ
ALCOHOL RATING: ●●○○○
STAR RATING: ★★★★★

Shake the ingredients together with ice and strain into the glass.
Alternatively, for a more modern serving, blend the ingredients with
a cup of ice and pour into the glass (pictured). Garnish with thin slices
of lime peel.

*An American engineer, Jennings Cox, invented the Daiquiri in Cuba in 1896. He
named the cocktail after the tin-mining town of Daiquiri, just outside Santiago.*

152 **moon shake**
1 ½ oz / 42 ml dark rum
1 oz / 28 ml Kalúha
1 tbsp lemon juice

GLASS TYPE: ϓ
ALCOHOL RATING: ●●○○○
STAR RATING: ★★★☆☆

Shake the ingredients together with ice and strain into the glass.
You can substitute the Kalúha with any flavoured liqueur of your choosing.

153 **passion daiquiri**
1 ½ oz / 42 ml light rum
juice of 1 lime
juice of ½ passion fruit (plus ½ for garnish)
1 tsp powdered (caster) sugar

GLASS TYPE: Y
ALCOHOL RATING: ●●○○○○
STAR RATING: ★★★★★

Shake all the ingredients together with ice and strain into the glass.
Squeeze the remaining half of the passion fruit over the drink and stir
in the pips to garnish.

The fresh passion fruit gives this daiquiri a sweet-and-sharp, fresh-fruit flavour.

154 **strawberry daiquiri**
1 oz / 28 g fresh strawberries
1 oz / 28 ml light rum
½ oz / 14 ml strawberry liqueur
1 oz / 28 ml lime juice
1 tsp powdered (caster) sugar

GLASS TYPE: Y
ALCOHOL RATING: ●●○○○○
STAR RATING: ★★★★★

Muddle the strawberries in a shaker. Add the remaining ingredients. Shake
with ice and strain into the glass. Alternatively, blend the ingredients
together with a cup of ice until smooth, and pour into the glass.

*This is a strawberry version of the Daiquiri (see opposite). If you don't have
strawberry liqueur, strawberry schnapps makes a good alternative. Today, the
blended version is more popular than the more traditional muddled version.*

155 **borinquen**
1 ½ oz / 42 ml light rum
1 oz / 28 ml lime juice
1 oz / 28 ml orange juice
1 tbsp passion fruit syrup
1 tsp 151-proof rum

GLASS TYPE: ▢
ALCOHOL RATING: ●●○○○○
STAR RATING: ★★★★★

At low speed, blend all of the ingredients (except for the 151-proof rum)
together with half a cup of crushed ice. Pour the mix into a glass. Float the
151-proof rum on top. Put a loose twist of lime and a loose twist of orange
inside the glass to garnish.

The 151-proof rum top gives this sweet and fruity cocktail an extra kick.

156 **rum daisy**
2 oz / 56 ml light rum
juice of ½ lemon
1 tsp grenadine
½ tsp powdered (caster) sugar

GLASS TYPE: ▢
ALCOHOL RATING: ●●○○○
STAR RATING: ★★★☆☆

Shake all the ingredients together with ice and strain into a glass half filled
with ice. Put a slice each of lemon, lime and kiwi into the drink to garnish.

*A daisy can be made with any base spirit, but the mix must contain lemon or lime
juice, as well as grenadine or a sweet liqueur. A small amount of soda is sometimes
added. This daisy is sweet-tasting with a hint of sourness.*

about the Bacardi Cocktail

The Bacardi Company invented this cocktail in the early 1900s. With its seductive style and flawless balance of flavours, the drink was an instant classic – synonymous with wealthy indulgence.

The Bacardi Cocktail is in fact the only cocktail to have a branded spirit in its name and that same branded spirit in its essential ingredients. During the Prohibition years in the US, when all alcohol was outlawed and the only drinking to be done was illicit and usually with rough, bootleg liquor, the Bacardi Cocktail was often mixed with any rum going. However, the Bacardi Company, who marketed their brand as a sophisticated drink, took exception to the continuation of this practice past the end of the liquor ban in 1933, and in particular when it continued in some of the country's swankiest establishments. The company took the case to court and, in 1936, the Supreme Court ruled in their favour, judging that any drink named a Bacardi Cocktail must contain Bacardi rum. This landmark victory served the company well (they had billboards across the States proclaiming the ruling). Despite being the epitome of cool during and after Prohibition and until as recently as the 1970s, the Bacardi Cocktail has suffered something of a dip in popularity in more recent years. Nevertheless, this cocktail is a true classic in terms of taste and appearance, so try one for old time's sake – I bet you enjoy it!

Bacardi Cocktail

2 ½ oz / 70 ml Bacardi light rum
¾ oz / 21 ml lime juice
½ oz / 14 ml grenadine

GLASS TYPE: 🍸
ALCOHOL RATING: ●●○○○
STAR RATING: ★★★★☆

Shake all of the ingredients together with ice and strain into the glass.
Decorate with a fresh, stemmed cherry.

158 midnight express

1 ½ oz / 42 ml dark rum
½ oz / 14 ml triple sec
¾ oz / 21 ml lime juice
splash sour mix (see p.17)
1 tsp egg white (optional; see p.16)

GLASS TYPE: ▢
ALCOHOL RATING: ●●○○○
STAR RATING: ★★★★☆

Shake all the ingredients together with ice and strain into an ice-filled glass.
This sour is made with lime and triple sec rather than lemon and sugar.

159 night cap

2 oz / 56 ml light rum
1 tsp powdered (caster) sugar
milk (warm)

GLASS TYPE: ▢
ALCOHOL RATING: ●●○○○
STAR RATING: ★★★★☆

Pour the rum and sugar into an old-fashioned glass, or an Irish coffee
glass if you have one. Fill with milk and stir. To garnish, lightly sprinkle
with nutmeg.
This drink is a great sleep-inducer – try it after a stressful day.

160 Bermuda Triangle

1 oz / 28 ml spiced rum
½ oz / 14 ml peach schnapps
3 oz / 84 ml orange juice

GLASS TYPE: ▢
ALCOHOL RATING: ●◐○○
STAR RATING: ★★★☆☆

Pour the ingredients into a glass filled with ice.
*Spiced rum is flavoured with spices and herbs, such as cinnamon, pepper
and vanilla. If you can't get hold of it, use gold rum and a pinch of cinnamon.*

161 white lily

1 oz / 28 ml light rum
¾ oz / 21 ml gin
¾ oz / 21 ml triple sec
¼ tsp Pernod

GLASS TYPE: ▽
ALCOHOL RATING: ●●●○○
STAR RATING: ★★★★★

Shake all the ingredients together with ice and strain into the glass.
Garnish with any edible flower of your choice.
*The gin adds herbal notes to this sweet drink, and the Pernod gives it
a liquorice finish.*

162 palmetto

1 ½ oz / 42 ml light rum
1 ½ oz / 42 ml dry vermouth
2 dashes orange bitters

GLASS TYPE: ▽
ALCOHOL RATING: ●●●○○
STAR RATING: ★★★★★

Pour the ingredients into a shaker, stir with ice and strain into the glass.
Dangle a loose orange twist from the rim of the glass to garnish.
This is a distinctively dry and herbal cocktail.

163   rum swizzle

juice of 1 lime
1 tsp powdered (caster) sugar
4 oz / 112 ml soda
2 dashes Angostura bitters
2 oz / 56 ml light or dark rum

GLASS TYPE: ▯
ALCOHOL RATING: ●●◐○○
STAR RATING: ★★★★★

Pour the lime juice, sugar and 2 oz/56 ml of soda into a highball. Fill the glass with ice and stir. Add the bitters and rum. Top with the remaining soda. Serve with a swizzle stick.

Originating in the West Indies in the early 1800s, a swizzle is made with spirit, lime juice, sugar or a liqueur, and sometimes soda. Small quantities of other ingredients are added for colour or flavour. The drink is served with a swizzle stick, so that the drinker can stir the mix to dissolve the sugar and sweeten the drink.

164   mojito

10 mint leaves
dash sugar syrup
2 oz / 56 ml Havana Club
soda

GLASS TYPE: ▯
ALCOHOL RATING: ●●○○○
STAR RATING: ★★★★★

Muddle the mint with the sugar in a higball glass. Fill the glass with crushed ice and pour in the rum. Top with soda. Garnish with a sprig of mint.

This refreshing Cuban cocktail tastes great with a float of dark rum.

165   New Orleans buck

1 ½ oz / 42 ml light rum
1 oz / 28 ml orange juice
½ oz / 14 ml lemon juice
ginger ale

GLASS TYPE: ▯
ALCOHOL RATING: ●●○○○
STAR RATING: ★★★★☆

Shake the first 3 ingredients together with ice and strain into an ice-filled glass. Top with ginger ale and stir. Place 2 slices of orange (halved) and 2 slices of lemon (halved) inside the glass to garnish.

The sweet rum, sharp fruit and spicy ginger create a perfect balance of tastes.

166   cocomacoque

1 ½ oz / 42 ml light rum
1 tsp coconut rum
2 oz / 56 ml orange juice
2 oz / 56 ml pineapple juice
juice of ½ lemon
1 tsp coconut milk
1 oz / 28 ml red wine

GLASS TYPE: ▯
ALCOHOL RATING: ●●○○○
STAR RATING: ★★★☆☆

Shake all the ingredients (except for the wine) together with ice. Pour the mix into an ice-filled glass. Top with wine. To garnish, put a pineapple stick inside the glass and sprinkle coconut flakes on top of the drink.

The red wine adds a hint of richness to this fruit-tasting cocktail.

151-proof passion

1 ¼ oz / 35 ml light rum
½ oz / 14 ml 151-proof rum
1 oz / 28 ml lime juice
1 oz / 28 ml orange juice
1 tbsp passion fruit syrup
½ fresh passion fruit (for the pips)

GLASS TYPE: ♟
ALCOHOL RATING: ●●◗○○
STAR RATING: ★★★★☆

Blend all the ingredients together (except for the passion fruit). Add half a cup of crushed ice and blend again, at a low speed. Pour the mix into the glass. Squeeze the passion fruit over the drink and stir in the pips to garnish.

Once you blend a cocktail with ice you will temper the taste of the alcohol. The result is a less forceful drink than you would normally expect from this much high-proof rum.

168 melon man

1 ¼ oz / 35 ml 151-proof rum
¾ oz / 21 ml Midori
4 oz / 112 ml orange juice

GLASS TYPE: ▯
ALCOHOL RATING: ●●●○○
STAR RATING: ★★☆☆☆

Pour the ingredients into a shaker, shake with ice and strain into an ice-filled glass. Place 2 thin slices of melon inside the glass to garnish.
This is a strong cocktail, which should be greeny-orange in colour.

169▼ pink paradise

1 oz / 28 ml rum
½ oz / 14 ml coconut rum
1 oz / 28 ml amaretto
3 oz / 84 ml cranberry juice
1 ½ oz / 42 ml pineapple juice

GLASS TYPE: ▯ ▯
ALCOHOL RATING: ●●○○○
STAR RATING: ★★★★★

Pour the ingredients into an old-fashioned glass filled with ice. Garnish with a pineapple wedge and a cherry.
You can also try this cocktail with fresh fruit: muddle 4 fresh cranberries in a shaker. Add the rum, amaretto and pineapple; shake and strain into an ice-filled highball.

banana cow

170

1 oz / 28 ml dark rum
1 oz / 28 ml crème de banane
1 ½ oz / 42 ml single cream
dash sugar syrup

GLASS TYPE: ▽
ALCOHOL RATING: ●●○○○
STAR RATING: ★★★☆☆

Shake all of the ingredients together with ice and strain into the glass. To garnish, place a slice of banana inside the glass and sprinkle nutmeg on top of the drink.

This cocktail also tastes good blended with milk instead of cream: blend the rum, crème de banane and sugar together with half a cup of milk and a cup of ice, and pour the mix into the glass. Garnish as before.

Quaker's cocktail

171

4 fresh raspberries
1 oz / 28 ml light rum
¼ oz / 7 ml brandy
juice of ¼ lemon
2 tsp raspberry syrup

GLASS TYPE: ▽
ALCOHOL RATING: ●○○○○
STAR RATING: ★★★★☆

Muddle the raspberries in a shaker. Add the remaining ingredients, shake with ice and strain into the glass.

The raspberry syrup helps to bring out the flavour of the fresh raspberries, and the mix of the syrup and the brandy enhances the sweetness of the rum.

Hurricane Leah

172

1 ½ oz / 42 ml light rum
¼ oz / 7 ml gin
¼ oz / 7 ml tequila
¼ oz / 7 ml vodka
dash blue curaçao
dash cherry brandy
3 oz / 84 ml orange juice

GLASS TYPE: ▯
ALCOHOL RATING: ●●●●○
STAR RATING: ★★★★★

Pour all the ingredients into a glass filled with ice and stir. To garnish, place a fresh cherry, an orange wheel and a lime wedge on the rim of the glass.

This rum iced tea is a lethal mix.

Robson

173

1 oz / 28 ml Jamaica dark rum
1 tbsp orange juice
2 tsp lemon juice
1 ½ tsp grenadine

GLASS TYPE: ▯
ALCOHOL RATING: ●○○○○
STAR RATING: ★★★☆☆

Shake all the ingredients together with ice and strain into an ice-filled glass. Put an orange wheel inside the glass to garnish.

The grenadine enhances the sweetness of the rich rum, which is balanced by the fresh orange and sharp lemon, to create a rounded drink.

caipirinha

1 lime (cut into eighths)
2 tsp sugar (brown)
2 oz / 56 ml cachaça

GLASS TYPE: ⊡
ALCOHOL RATING: ●●○○○
STAR RATING: ★★★★★

Muddle the lime together with the sugar in an old-fashioned glass. Fill the glass with crushed ice. Pour in the cachaça and stir. Top with more crushed ice.

MODERN CLASSIC

about the caipirinha

The piquant Caipirinha is an upbeat party drink designed to transport you straight to the nearest carnival, fiesta or beach party. The drink is made from cachaça – a Brazilian rum distilled directly from sugar-cane juice and similar in taste to light rum.

The origins of the Caipirinha itself are unclear, but cachaça was first distilled in 1532 after the Portuguese settlers brought sugar cane to Brazil from Madeira. In Brazil today consumption of the spirit runs a close second only to beer consumption (a billion litres of cachaça are produced each year and the country has more than 4,000 brands) and is widely agreed to be Brazil's national drink.

Traditionally, white sugar is used to make the Caipirinha rather than brown (as I have suggested). However, as Brazilian white sugar is more coarse than white sugar found elsewhere in the world (especially that in Europe and the US), I think that brown sugar is a closer, more authentic match for the original Brazilian blend.

planter's punch no. 1
2 oz / 56 ml light rum
juice of 1 lime
juice of ½ lemon
juice of ½ orange
1 tsp pineapple juice
1 oz / 28 ml Jamaica dark rum
2 dashes triple sec
dash grenadine

GLASS TYPE: ▯
ALCOHOL RATING: ●●●◐○
STAR RATING: ★★★★★

Pour the first 5 ingredients into a glass filled with ice. Stir until the glass is frosted. Add the Jamaica dark rum and stir again. Top with triple sec and grenadine. Garnish with a slice each of orange, lemon, lime and pineapple, and a sprig of mint. You could even add a cherry if desired.

Jamaica dark rum is full-bodied, with a mellow caramel flavour, which works well in this sweet and fruity Caribbean mix. This drink makes the perfect winter punch – try it at your Christmas and New Year parties.

176 **planter's punch no. 2**

juice of 2 limes
2 oz / 56 ml soda
2 tsp powdered (caster) sugar
2 ½ oz / 70 ml light rum
2 dashes Angostura bitters
dash grenadine

GLASS TYPE: ▯
ALCOHOL RATING: ●●◑○○
STAR RATING: ★★★★☆

Pour the first 3 ingredients into a glass filled with ice. Stir until the glass is frosted. Add the rum and bitters. Stir again. Top with grenadine. Place a sprig of mint and a fresh cherry inside the glass to garnish.

This punch is a drier version of the Planter's Punch no. 1 (see opposite), it is made without the Jamaica dark rum or an abundance of fruit juices.

177 **Mississippi planter's punch**

1 oz / 28 ml light rum
¼ oz / 7 ml bourbon
¼ oz / 7 ml brandy
juice of 1 lemon
1 tbsp powdered (caster) sugar
soda

GLASS TYPE: ▯
ALCOHOL RATING: ●●◑○○
STAR RATING: ★★★★☆

Shake all of the ingredients (except for the soda) together with ice and strain into an ice-filled glass. Fill with soda and stir. Put 3 slices of lemon inside the glass to garnish.

Watch out – this mix of light and dark spirits will have a stronger effect on you than you might expect. You may want to add a dash of sugar syrup to sweeten.

178 **Sir Walter**

¾ oz / 21 ml light rum
¾ oz / 21 ml brandy
1 tsp triple sec
1 tsp grenadine
1 tsp lemon juice

GLASS TYPE: ▽
ALCOHOL RATING: ●◑○○○
STAR RATING: ★★☆☆☆

Pour all of the ingredients into a shaker, shake with ice and strain into the glass.

This rich and warming drink tastes largely of rum, but with a hint of brandy.

179 **Beachcomber**

1 ½ oz / 42 ml light rum
½ oz / 14 ml triple sec
1 oz / 28 ml sour mix (see p.17)
½ oz / 14 ml grenadine

GLASS TYPE: ▽
ALCOHOL RATING: ●●○○○
STAR RATING: ★★★☆☆

Shake all of the ingredients together with ice and strain into a sugar-rimmed glass. Put a loose lime twist inside the glass to garnish.

This after dinner cocktail is sweet-tasting, with a hint of sourness.

180 ▲ piña colada

3 oz / 84 ml light rum
3 tbsp coconut milk
dash pineapple juice
½ handful of fresh pineapple (chopped)
dash sugar syrup (optional)

GLASS TYPE: 🍸
ALCOHOL RATING: ●●●○○
STAR RATING: ★★★★★

Blend all the ingredients at high speed with a cup of crushed ice until smooth. Pour the mix into the glass. Garnish with a pineapple wedge and 3 pineapple leaves.

This famous mix was probably invented by bartender Ramon Marrero in 1954 at the Caribe Hilton Hotel in Puerto Rico. The Piña Colada headed the trend for blended cocktails.

blue Hawaiian

181

1 oz / 28 ml light rum
1 oz / 28 ml coconut rum
1 oz / 28 ml blue curaçao
2 oz / 56 ml pineapple juice

GLASS TYPE: ⬡
ALCOHOL RATING: ●●○○○
STAR RATING: ★★★★☆

Blend all the ingredients at high speed with a cup of crushed ice
until smooth. Pour the mix into the glass. Attach a slice of pineapple and
a cherry to the rim of the glass to garnish.

*A blue version of the Piña Colada (see opposite). The sweet coconut rum goes
well with the clean-tasting light rum.*

torridora

182

1 ½ oz / 42 ml light rum
½ oz / 14 ml Kalúha
1 ½ tsp single cream
1 tsp 151-proof rum

GLASS TYPE: 🍸
ALCOHOL RATING: ●●○○○
STAR RATING: ★★★★☆

Shake the first 3 ingredients together with ice and strain into the glass.
Float the 151-proof rum on top. Place 3 coffee beans on top of the drink
to garnish.

*You can also make a Torridora Cappuccino by adding a single espresso: pour
the espresso into a shaker, then add the listed ingredients; shake and strain
into the glass. Garnish as before.*

pineapple fizz

183

2 oz / 56 ml light rum
1 oz / 28 ml pineapple juice
½ tsp powdered (caster) sugar
soda

GLASS TYPE: ⬡
ALCOHOL RATING: ●●○○○
STAR RATING: ★★★☆☆

Shake the first 3 ingredients together with ice and strain into an ice-filled
glass. Fill with soda and stir. Cut 10 fingertip-sized cubes of fresh
pineapple and drop them into the drink to garnish.

Try topping this drink with ginger ale instead of soda to create a spicy fizz.

Cuba libre

184

2 oz / 56 ml Havana Club or gold rum
cola
3 lime wedges

GLASS TYPE: ⬡
ALCOHOL RATING: ●●○○○
STAR RATING: ★★★★★

Pour the rum into a glass filled with ice. Top with cola. Squeeze the juice of
the lime wedges into the glass and stir. Drop the spent lime wedges into the
drink to garnish.

*Legend has it that this cocktail originated in the late 19th century, toward the end of
the Spanish-American war. In a bar in old Havana, a US army officer mixed rum with
the new soft drink cola, and named it "Cuba Libre", which translated into English
means "Free Cuba".*

the whiskies

Whisky (and whiskey; see p.114) has a distinguished history dating back many hundreds of years – perhaps even to as early as the 6th century CE. Whisk(e)y was first made in Scotland or Ireland (precise provenance is unclear). In the 17th century, Scottish and Irish settlers took their distillation expertise with them to America, where different soils and climates forced them to adapt their spirit-making techniques to give us the myriad styles of whisk(e)y found today. Whiskies are made by distilling and maturing fermented cereal grain. The type of grain used (including corn, rye, barley and wheat), as well as the soil in which the grain grows, define its character.

This chapter is divided in two. The first half is devoted to bourbon, an American whiskey of a comparatively fruity and vanilla-like flavour, which is highly popular as a cocktail base. The second section presents cocktails made with a variety of other whiskies, notably blended scotch and Irish. Throughout this chapter I have selected the whisk(e)y that I think best suits the drink. However, by all means experiment using different whiskies in different blends.

Bourbon

A distinctive American whiskey, bourbon can be called bourbon only if it contains a minimum of 51% corn (maize). The whiskey originates from Bourbon County, Kentucky, which to this day remains the centre of most of the US bourbon industry, although the spirit may now be distilled anywhere in the US.

Bourbon was first distilled in the late 18th century by Scottish Presbyterian immigrants who, having arrived in the new world, moved westward to Kentucky from Pennsylvania – taking their whiskey-distilling techniques with them. In Pennsylvania the whiskey had been made from rye, but the soil of Kentucky was better suited to growing corn.

Today, most bourbon contains more than the required 51% corn. The remainder of the drink is distilled from rye and malted barley. Any differences in the proportions can make for slight variations in the character of each blend. However, the maturation process is thought to be responsible for producing bourbon's unique flavour, which is sweeter than other whiskies. The spirit is stored in single-use, charred new American oak barrels, which are particularly high in flavourings such as vanilla, for at least two years (other whiskies are matured in re-usable barrels).

185 Southern lady

2 oz / 56 ml bourbon
1 oz / 28 ml Southern Comfort
½ oz / 14 ml parfait amour
3 oz / 84 pineapple juice
dash sugar syrup
2 oz / 56 ml soda
1 oz / 28 ml lime juice

GLASS TYPE: ▯
ALCOHOL RATING: ●●●◑○
STAR RATING: ★★★★☆

Shake the first 5 ingredients together with ice and strain into a glass half filled with ice. Top with soda and lime juice. To decorate, place a wedge of pineapple and a cherry on the rim of the glass.
The sour lime will hit the taste buds first, followed by the sweet pineapple. The parfait amour will give the whole drink a fresh lavender aroma. This is the perfect mix for lazy summer afternoons.

186 Kentucky colonel

1 ½ oz / 42 ml bourbon
½ oz / 14 ml Bénédictine

GLASS TYPE: Y
ALCOHOL RATING: ●●○○○
STAR RATING: ★★★★☆

Stir the ingredients together with ice and strain into the glass. Place
a lemon peel inside the glass to garnish.

*The sweet, herbal Bénédictine makes a great digestive, and is believed by many to
be the world's oldest liqueur – first distilled in 1510 by Italian Bénédictine monks.*

187 double entendre

1 fresh apricot (plus 1 for garnish)
2 sugar cubes (brown)
2 oz / 56 ml bourbon
dash apricot brandy
soda

GLASS TYPE: □
ALCOHOL RATING: ●●○○○
STAR RATING: ★★★★☆

Muddle the apricot with the sugar in a shaker. Add the bourbon and
the brandy, and shake with ice. Strain the mix into a glass filled with
crushed ice. Top with soda. To garnish, slice the remaining apricot into
6 pieces and add to the drink.

This mix was created in the late 1990s by Elliot Isaacs in Bill's Bar, Tokyo.

188 red-hot passion

½ oz / 14 ml bourbon
½ oz / 14 ml amaretto
½ oz / 14 ml Southern Comfort
¼ oz / 7 ml sloe gin
splash triple sec
splash grenadine
splash orange juice
splash pineapple juice

GLASS TYPE: □
ALCOHOL RATING: ●●◑○○
STAR RATING: ★★★★☆

Pour all of the ingredients into a glass filled with ice. Stir gently. Place
an orange wheel and 2 fresh cherries on the rim of the glass to decorate.

*Although this sweet mix contains fruit juice, it is a rich and strong-tasting cocktail.
Try topping with lemonade to give it a fizz and to temper the alcohol.*

189 pulling bear

2 oz / 56 ml bourbon
¾ oz / 21 ml triple sec
1 tbsp apricot brandy
juice of ½ lime

GLASS TYPE: Y
ALCOHOL RATING: ●●◑○○
STAR RATING: ★★★☆☆

Shake all of the ingredients together with ice and strain into the glass. Place
a peel of orange inside the glass to garnish.

*The bourbon and triple sec combine to create a sweet orange flavour. Try using
fresh orange juice instead of triple sec for a fruitier and less alcoholic alternative.*

190   **mint julep (Southern style)**
2 tsp powdered (caster) sugar
2 tsp water (cold)
2 ½ oz / 70 ml bourbon

GLASS TYPE: ⬜
ALCOHOL RATING: ●●◕○○
STAR RATING: ★★★★★

Pour the sugar and the water into the glass. Stir until the sugar is dissolved. Pour in the bourbon and add 2 ice cubes. Stir, adding more ice until the glass is filled. Place 5 or 6 sprigs of mint on top of the ice to garnish. Serve with a straw.
The mint is used for aroma rather than taste in this shorter and stronger variation on the classic Mint Julep (see opposite).

191   **jocose julep**
2 oz / 56 ml bourbon
¼ oz / 7 ml crème de menthe (green)
1 oz / 28 ml lime juice
1 tsp sugar syrup
5 mint leaves (chopped)
soda

GLASS TYPE: ⬜
ALCOHOL RATING: ●●◔○○
STAR RATING: ★★★★☆

Blend the ingredients (except for the soda). Pour into a glass filled with ice and top with soda. Place a sprig of mint inside the glass to decorate.
On serving, this cocktail will have a frothy opaque-green head, which will slowly disappear, leaving a pale green drink containing hundreds of tiny pieces of mint – beware: the mint can get stuck in between your teeth!

192   **coffee old-fashioned**
1 ½ oz / 42 ml bourbon
½ oz / 14 ml crème de cacao (brown)
a single espresso (hot)
¼ cup water (cold)
2 tsp powdered (caster) sugar

GLASS TYPE: ⬜
ALCOHOL RATING: ●●○○○
STAR RATING: ★★★★☆

Shake all of the ingredients together with ice and strain into an ice-filled glass. Sprinkle freshly ground coffee granules on top of the drink to garnish.
For a frothy, citrus-flavoured version of this drink, add 2 dashes of orange bitters before you shake, then top with soda and slip in an orange slice.

193   **Allegheny**
1 oz / 28 ml bourbon
1 oz / 28 ml dry vermouth
1 ½ tsp crème de mûre
1 ½ tsp lemon juice

GLASS TYPE: 🍸
ALCOHOL RATING: ●●●○○
STAR RATING: ★★★☆☆

Shake all of the ingredients together with ice and strain into the glass. Place a lemon peel inside the glass to garnish.
Bourbon works well with all fruit flavours – try experimenting with different berry-flavoured liqueurs instead of the crème de mûre.

mint julep

4 sprigs mint (plus 1 for garnish)
1 tsp powdered (caster) sugar
2 tsp water (cold)
2 ½ oz / 70 ml bourbon

GLASS TYPE: ▯
ALCOHOL RATING: ●●●○○
STAR RATING: ★★★★★

Muddle the mint leaves together with the sugar and water in a highball. Fill the glass with crushed ice and pour in the bourbon. Slowly stir, adding more ice until the glass is filled with ice. Garnish with a sprig of mint.

TRADITIONAL CLASSIC

about the mint julep

The cocktail that truly characterizes the American South, this refreshing, sweet, bourbon drink immediately brings to mind Southern belles on hot summer days. This recipe dates back to the early 1800s but "julep" is a much older term, originating in Arabia, meaning a sweet, often medicinal, drink.

This cocktail is the traditional drink of the Kentucky Derby, held in May each year, when allegedly more than 80,000 Mint Juleps are served over the two-day celebration. The drink was originally presented in a sterling silver tankard, known as a "Julep cup", but in today's bars the Mint Julep is served in a highball glass.

There is continuous debate among bartenders about whether the mint in this cocktail should be muddled or stirred. I suggest that this depends on how minty you like your cocktail — muddling the mint will release its juices and produce a much mintier-tasting cocktail than a stirred version. But whatever your preference, for the ultimate thirst-quencher, chill the mixed cocktail in the refrigerator for 30 minutes before serving, and then sip slowly so that the ice melts gradually, making a longer drink.

195 Louisville cooler

1 ½ oz / 42 ml bourbon
1 oz / 28 ml orange juice
1 tbsp lime juice
1 tsp powdered (caster) sugar

GLASS TYPE: ▢
ALCOHOL RATING: ●◑○○○
STAR RATING: ★★☆☆☆

Shake all the ingredients together with ice and strain into an ice-filled glass.
Place a slice of orange inside the glass to garnish.
I'm told that this cocktail is a favourite among the local Jazz musicians of Louisville.

196▼ Southern belle

1 ¼ oz / 35 ml bourbon
¾ oz / 21 ml triple sec
8 oz / 224 ml pineapple juice
2 oz / 56 ml orange juice
1 slice fresh pineapple (chopped)
splash grenadine

GLASS TYPE: ▯
ALCOHOL RATING: ●●○○○
STAR RATING: ★★★★★

Shake all of the ingredients (except for the grenadine) vigorously with ice.
Strain the mix into an ice-filled glass and pour in the grenadine.
The grenadine sinks down to the bottom of the drink to give a beautiful sunset effect.

197 dixie

2 oz / 56 ml bourbon
¼ tsp crème de menthe (white)
¼ tsp triple sec
dash Angostura bitters
½ tsp powdered (caster) sugar

GLASS TYPE: ▽
ALCOHOL RATING: ●●◐○○
STAR RATING: ★★★☆☆

Shake all the ingredients together with ice and strain into the glass. Place a mint leaf inside the glass to garnish.

If, like me, you're not wild about crème de menthe, you can use fresh mint instead. Shake 5 leaves of fresh mint and a dash of sugar syrup together with the bourbon, triple sec and bitters. Strain the mix through a tea-strainer as, unlike the Jocose Julep (see no. 191), the final drink shouldn't contain pieces of mint.

198 bourbon cobbler

2 ½ oz / 70 ml bourbon
1 tbsp lemon juice
2 tsp grapefruit juice
½ tsp orgeat syrup

GLASS TYPE: ▯
ALCOHOL RATING: ●●◐○○
STAR RATING: ★★★☆☆

Shake all the ingredients together with ice and strain into an ice-filled glass. Place a wedge of peach inside the drink to garnish.

You can substitute the orgeat syrup with almond extract, which has a stronger flavour. This is a short version of a traditional cobbler, which is a long, stirred drink.

199 Sawichi

2 oz / 56 ml bourbon
dash crème de cacao (brown)
dash Frangelico
½ lime

GLASS TYPE: ▯
ALCOHOL RATING: ●●◐○○
STAR RATING: ★★★★★

Pour the first 3 ingredients into a glass filled with ice. Stir. Squeeze the lime over the drink and drop in the spent lime to garnish.

The sour lime cuts through the nutty, chocolate flavour, to create a more modern-tasting drink.

200 rasping red

6 oz / 170 g fresh raspberries
1 ½ oz / 42 ml bourbon
½ oz / 14 ml lemon juice
½ oz / 14 ml raspberry purée
dash sugar syrup

GLASS TYPE: ▯
ALCOHOL RATING: ●◐○○○
STAR RATING: ★★★★☆

Muddle the raspberries in a shaker. Pour in the remaining ingredients. Shake with ice and strain into a glass filled with crushed ice. To garnish, put a loose lemon twist inside the glass and drop in 2 raspberries.

This drink should be a beautiful burgundy colour. The lemon will add a citrus tang to this sour mix.

magnolia

201

1 ¼ oz / 35 ml bourbon
1 ¼ oz / 35 ml Grand Marnier
splash sugar syrup
splash soda

GLASS TYPE: ▯
ALCOHOL RATING: ●●◐○○○
STAR RATING: ★★★★★

Shake all the ingredients (except for the soda) together with ice. Strain
into an ice-filled glass and top with soda. Place a loose orange twist
inside the glass to garnish.

This sweet orange-flavoured cocktail is one of my favourite ways to start an evening.

Tennessee fizz

202

¼ oz / 7 ml bourbon
1 or 2 dashes Angostura bitters
½ tsp powdered (caster) sugar
champagne

GLASS TYPE: ▯
ALCOHOL RATING: ●●○○○○
STAR RATING: ★★★★★

Shake the bourbon together with the bitters and sugar and pour
into a glass filled with ice. Fill with champagne. Put 3 thin peach
slices into the drink to garnish.

*The garnish adds a sweet flavour to this herbal, dry mix. Be sure to use
a ripe peach.*

lonely hearts

203

1 ½ oz / 42 ml bourbon
1 ½ tsp apricot brandy
dash Angostura bitters
1 tbsp grapefruit juice
1 ½ tsp lemon juice

GLASS TYPE: ▼
ALCOHOL RATING: ●●●○○○
STAR RATING: ★★★☆☆

Shake all of the ingredients together with ice and strain into the glass.
To garnish, cut a slice of grapefruit and halve it. Place one half inside
the glass and the other on the rim.

This is a sweet-and-sour cocktail with a tangy edge.

Brighton punch

204

1 oz / 28 ml bourbon
¼ oz / 7 ml Bénédictine
¼ oz / 7 ml brandy
2 oz / 56 ml orange juice
juice of ½ lemon
soda

GLASS TYPE: ▯
ALCOHOL RATING: ●●◐○○○
STAR RATING: ★★★☆☆

Shake all of the ingredients (except for the soda) together with ice and pour
into a glass three-quarters filled with crushed ice. Top with soda and stir. Put
2 slices of orange and 2 slices of lemon into the drink to garnish.

*The Bénédictine enhances the sweet flavours of the bourbon, and the brandy
adds a smooth finish to the drink. This cocktail makes a great fruity party punch.*

ward 8

3 oz / 84 ml bourbon
1 oz / 28 ml lemon juice
1 oz / 28 ml orange juice
3 dashes grenadine

GLASS TYPE: ⏣
ALCOHOL RATING: ●●●○○
STAR RATING: ★★★★★

Pour the ingredients into a shaker. Shake with ice and strain into the glass.

TRADITIONAL CLASSIC

about the ward 8

Nothing whatever to do with hospital wards, the origins of this classic bourbon cocktail are to be found in 1890s downtown Boston. The story goes that in 1898, on the eve of a local election in the political district of Ward Eight, the Democrat candidate Martin Lomasney and his supporters gathered at their regular gentleman's club and requested a new drink for their pre-victory toast. The bartender took the popular cocktail base bourbon and mixed it with citrus juice and grenadine, thus mellowing the strong whiskey flavour. The mix surprised many by making a success of a bourbon and juice combination, something previously thought of as unpalatable by most bourbon drinkers.

Not often ordered today, the Ward 8 nevertheless remains true to its original recipe and this cocktail deserves its classic status for being one of the cornerstone drinks in the history of cocktails. So go on, give it a try and reacquaint yourself with an original classic.

other whiskies

A range of whiskies other than bourbon are also used as a base spirit in many cocktails. Most common are rye whiskey, Irish whiskey and blended scotch whisky (unblended scotch is drunk neat).

Most rye whiskey comes from the US and was probably first made in the 17th century by Scottish and Irish settlers who used rye as an alternative to the high-quality malting barley which they used to make whisk(e)y back home. Rye whiskey must contain at least 51% rye. Canadian rye whisky includes a range of cereal grains, such as corn, wheat, barley and malted barley. The blending of these grains is key to producing Canadian whisky's clean and soft flavours. Irish whiskey was probably first made in Medieval times, from a mix of barley, malted barley and other cereals. Most Irish whiskies are triple distilled (scotch is double distilled), which gives them a light, clean taste. Both Canadian and Irish whiskies must be oak-aged for a minimum of three years.

Scotch whisky is made from malted barley alone. A blended scotch contains upward of a dozen single malt whiskies, blended together with two or three grain whiskies to achieve a consistent, balanced taste.

For your reference, Scottish and Canadian whiskies are spelt without an "e" (although occasional Canadian blends include the "e") and Irish and US whiskies are spelt with an "e". Over the following pages, recipes listing "whiskey of choice" mean that you can use any kind of whiskey, including blended scotch.

206 **rickety lime**
2 oz / 56 ml whiskey of choice
juice of ½ lime
soda

GLASS TYPE: ▯
ALCOHOL RATING: ●●○○○
STAR RATING: ★★☆☆☆

Pour the whiskey and the lime into a glass filled with ice. Fill with soda and stir. Place a tight twist of lime inside the glass to garnish.
This cocktail is similar to the Irish Ricky (see no.216). However, using lime rather than lemon creates a slightly cleaner and more acidic drink.

207 **Bennett sour**
2 oz / 56 ml whiskey of choice
½ oz / 14 ml Bénédictine
1 oz / 28 ml sour mix (see p.17)
dash egg white (optional)

GLASS TYPE: ▢
ALCOHOL RATING: ●●○○○
STAR RATING: ★★☆☆☆

Shake all of the ingredients together with ice and strain into an ice-filled glass. To garnish, drop a slice of lemon and a cherry into the glass.
The Bénédictine liqueur will give this sour a distinctive, herbal flavour. This is a sweeter version of the scotch Whiskey Sour (see no.224) The inclusion of egg white is, of course, your decision (see p.16).

208 **red daisy**
2 oz / 56 ml whiskey of choice
juice of ½ lemon
1 tsp grenadine
½ tsp powdered (caster) sugar

GLASS TYPE: ▢
ALCOHOL RATING: ●●○○○
STAR RATING: ★★★☆☆

Shake all of the ingredients together with ice and strain into the glass. Add an ice cube. Place a slice of lemon and a slice of orange inside the glass to garnish.
This is the whiskey version of the daisy (see Rum Daisy, no.156). The grenadine will add a hint of sweetness to the whiskey.

209 **Lawhill**
1 ¾ oz / 49 ml rye whiskey
½ oz / 14 ml dry vermouth
¼ tsp Pernod
dash Angostura bitters
½ tsp maraschino

GLASS TYPE: ▽
ALCOHOL RATING: ●●●○○
STAR RATING: ★★★★☆

Pour all the ingredients into a shaker. Stir with ice and strain into the glass.
The Pernod blends well with the other flavours in this cocktail to form a dry drink.

210 **whiskey smash**
4 sprigs mint
2 sugar cubes (brown)
1 oz / 28 ml soda
2 oz / 56 ml whiskey of choice

GLASS TYPE: ▢
ALCOHOL RATING: ●●○○○
STAR RATING: ★★★★☆

Muddle the mint together with the sugar and soda in an old-fashioned glass. Pour in the whiskey. Add crushed ice and stir.
This great summer cooler is a whiskey variation on the classic bourbon-based Mint Julep (see no.194).

about the old-fashioned

Just about the smoothest and most drinkable whiskey cocktail you might ever find, the Old-fashioned is a traditional classic and is named after the glass in which it is served.

Legend has it that the Old-fashioned was first created in the early 20th century in the Pendennis Club in Louisville, Kentucky, for a retired general who wasn't keen on whiskey. The sweetness of the sugar, the bitter Angostura and the citrus twist, along with a generous quantity of ice, softened the harsh flavour of the whiskey. This pleased the general and the Old-fashioned quickly became a cocktail menu staple.

The mark of a good Old-fashioned and, indeed, of a good bartender, lies in the skillful preparation of the drink. Making this cocktail is a slow process – the drink should take at least five minutes to mix. The Old-fashioned should never be shaken: the ingredients should be stirred together slowly, allowing the glass to frost up during the process. The cocktail should be drunk as it has been mixed – slowly and with deliberation, savouring every drop. If there is no ice left by the end of the glass, you should have captured the mood and the taste of this drink at its best.

old-fashioned

2 sugar cubes (white)
2 dashes Angostura bitters
orange peel
2 oz / 56 ml whiskey of choice

GLASS TYPE: ○
ALCOHOL RATING: ●●○○○
STAR RATING: ★★★★★

Place the sugar cubes in an old-fashioned glass and pour the bitters on to the cubes, to soak them in bitters. Add the orange peel and a dash of whiskey. Muddle the ingredients. Stir the mix and as you do so slowly pour in the remaining whiskey. Continue to stir and add ice until the glass is frosted and filled with ice (this should take at least 5 minutes; see opposite). Drop in a cherry to garnish.

Try mixing this cocktail with bourbon for a sweeter, barrel flavour:

John Collins

212

2 oz / 56 ml whiskey of choice
juice of ½ lemon
1 tsp powdered (caster) sugar
soda

GLASS TYPE:

ALCOHOL RATING: ●●○○○

STAR RATING: ★★★★★

Shake the first 3 ingredients together with ice and strain into an ice-filled glass. Fill with soda and stir. Garnish with a loose orange twist, a slice of lemon and a cherry.

TRADITIONAL CLASSIC

about the John Collins

The John Collins and the Tom Collins (see no.57) are known as "the Brothers", being the oldest of the collins clan which includes almost any base spirit that is mixed with lemon, sugar and soda water and served in a collins (highball) glass. The gin-based Tom Collins is thought to have been created by bartender John Collins, inviting confusion between the two drinks and their names. The John Collins can also be made with bourbon. It's a good idea to specify your prefered base spirit when ordering a John Collins at a bar.

213 **commodore**

2 oz / 56 ml whiskey of choice
2 dashes orange bitters
juice of ½ lime or ¼ lemon
dash sugar syrup

GLASS TYPE: ☐
ALCOHOL RATING: ●●○○○
STAR RATING: ★★★☆☆

Shake all the ingredients with ice and strain into the glass. Place a tight
orange twist inside the glass to garnish.
This cocktail is a sour and easy-to-make alternative to the classic Old-fashioned
(see no.211).

214 **Rory O'More**

2 oz / 56 ml Irish whiskey
½ oz / 14 ml sweet vermouth
dash orange bitters

GLASS TYPE: ☐
ALCOHOL RATING: ●●○○○
STAR RATING: ★★★★☆

Pour the ingredients into a shaker, stir with ice and strain into the glass.
Put a peel of orange inside the glass to garnish.
You can really taste the smooth, clean taste of the Irish whiskey in this mix.
However, this cocktail has lost popularity in recent years and is yet to enjoy the
contemporary recognition that it deserves.

215 **Irish lemonade**

2 oz / 56 ml Irish whiskey
juice of 1 lemon
juice of 1 lime
½ tsp grenadine
1 tbsp powdered (caster) sugar
soda

GLASS TYPE: ☐
ALCOHOL RATING: ●●○○○
STAR RATING: ★★★☆☆

Shake the first 5 ingredients together with ice and strain into a glass filled
with crushed ice. Fill with soda and drop in a cherry to garnish.
Try topping this drink with apple juice as well as soda for a more refreshing flavour.

216 **Irish Rickey**

1 ½ oz / 42 ml Irish whiskey
juice of ½ lemon
soda

GLASS TYPE: ☐
ALCOHOL RATING: ●○○○○
STAR RATING: ★★★☆☆

Pour the whiskey and the lemon juice into a glass filled with ice.
Fill with soda and stir. Place a slice of lime inside the glass to garnish.
You may wish to add a dash of sugar syrup to sweeten this sour rickey.
(See no.95 for the traditional Gin Rickey.)

about the Sazerac

One of the world's oldest cocktails, the Sazerac originates in early 19th-century New Orleans. Creole apothecary, Antoine Péychaud, who invented Péychaud bitters in 1793, set up a pharmacy in the city's French Quarter. Péychaud's bitters was thought to aid digestion and promote good health, and Péychaud would mix his bitters together with brandy and sugar and serve the cocktail to friends and customers. In the 1850s an agent of Sazerac cognacs, John B. Schiller, opened the Sazerac Coffee House (a drinking establishment) just along the street from Péychaud's pharmacy. Schiller began to serve Péychaud's popular mix, which he made exclusively with the imported Sazerac brandy, and the cocktail became known as the Sazerac.

In the 1870s there was a change in ownership at the Sazerac Coffee House, which lead to alterations in the Sazerac's ingredients. Rye whiskey replaced brandy as the cocktail's base spirit, and absinthe was added to the recipe. When absinthe was widely banned in the early 20th century, Pernod was used as a substitute. Today, Péychaud's bitters are rarely available and so Angostura bitters are most commonly used instead.

Despite the evolution over the years, the Sazerac remains a powerful drink, traditionally served without ice. You may wish to top the drink with soda for a more refreshing, easier-to-drink version. If you are a fan of anise you could discard only half the amount of Pernod (see method).

Sazerac

½ oz / 14 ml Pernod
dash Angostura bitters
2 dashes sugar syrup
2 oz / 56 ml rye whiskey

GLASS TYPE: ▢
ALCOHOL RATING: ●●◐○○
STAR RATING: ★★★★★

Swirl the Pernod in a chilled, ice-filled glass, to line the ice with Pernod.
Discard the Pernod and add the bitters and sugar syrup. Stir. Pour in the
whiskey. Garnish with a peel of orange.

218 Irish coffee

1 ½ oz / 42 ml Irish whiskey
a double espresso (hot)
2 oz / 56 ml water (boiling)
dash sugar syrup
¼ oz / 7 ml double cream

GLASS TYPE: ♀
ALCOHOL RATING: ●◐○○○
STAR RATING: ★★★★★

Pour the first 4 ingredients into a large wine glass, or an Irish coffee
glass if you have one, and stir. Float the cream on top. Garnish with
3 coffee beans.

Variations on this recipe include tequila, brandy and cream-based liqueur versions.
Simply substitute the whiskey with your chosen spirit or liqueur.

219 Tipperary

2 oz / 56 ml Irish whiskey
½ oz / 14 ml Chartreuse (green)
¼ oz / 7 ml sweet vermouth

GLASS TYPE: ♈
ALCOHOL RATING: ●●●◐○
STAR RATING: ★★☆☆☆

Pour the ingredients into a shaker. Stir with ice and strain into the glass.
Drop in a cherry to garnish.

This is an incredibly strong cocktail – there's only the ice to temper the alcohol.

220 Shillelagh

2 oz / 56 ml Irish whiskey
1 tbsp light rum
1 tbsp sloe gin
juice of ½ lemon
dash sugar syrup
lemonade

GLASS TYPE: ▢
ALCOHOL RATING: ●●○○○
STAR RATING: ★★★★☆

Shake all the ingredients (except for the lemonade) together with ice and
strain into an ice-filled glass. Top with lemonade. To garnish, drop 2 fresh
cherries, 2 raspberries, 2 strawberries and 2 slices of peach inside
the drink.

This is an excellent whiskey punch, which can be served to any whiskey lover.

221 Irish toad

2 oz / 56 ml Irish whiskey
1 tsp Chartreuse (green)
1 tsp crème de menthe (green)

GLASS TYPE: ♈
ALCOHOL RATING: ●●◐○○
STAR RATING: ★☆☆☆☆

Pour the ingredients into a shaker. Stir with ice and strain into the glass.
To garnish, place a sprig of mint inside the glass, or drop in an olive.

On drinking this cocktail you will experience a distinct minty taste, followed by
a burning sensation from the Chartreuse. I've tried this concoction once – but
never again!

222 ward eight

2 oz / 56 ml blended scotch
juice of ½ lemon
1 tsp grenadine
1 tsp powdered (caster) sugar

GLASS TYPE: ▢
ALCOHOL RATING: ●●○○○
STAR RATING: ★★★★☆

Shake all of the ingredients together with ice and strain into a glass filled with crushed ice. Place a slice of orange, a slice of lemon and a cherry inside the glass to garnish.

This is the scotch version of the classic bourbon-based Ward 8 (see no.205). For a stronger-tasting alternative, pour all of the ingredients into a glass filled with ice and stir (this version is designed to be sipped slowly).

223 algonquin

1 ½ oz / 42 ml blended scotch
1 oz / 28 ml dry vermouth
1 oz / 28 ml pineapple juice

GLASS TYPE: ▽
ALCOHOL RATING: ●●○○○
STAR RATING: ★★★★☆

Pour the ingredients into a shaker, shake with ice and strain into the glass. Place a pineapple leaf inside the glass to garnish.

For a fresher and fruitier cocktail, try shaking this blend with a slice of fresh pineapple instead of the juice. Garnish with a pineapple stick.

224 whisky sour

2 oz / 56 ml blended scotch
juice of ½ lemon
½ tsp powdered (caster) sugar
1 tsp egg white (optional)

GLASS TYPE: ▢
ALCOHOL RATING: ●●○○○
STAR RATING: ★★★★★

Shake all of the ingredients with ice and strain into an ice-filled glass. To garnish, place a slice of lemon and a cherry inside the glass.

This is my personal favourite of all the sours. If you choose to include egg white (see Vodka Sour; no.11), your drink will have a smoother consistency and a foamy head. You can substitute the scotch with bourbon for a sweeter version.

225 double standard sour

1 oz / 28 ml blended scotch
½ oz / 14 ml gin
juice of 1 lime or ½ lemon
½ tsp grenadine
½ tsp powdered (caster) sugar

GLASS TYPE: ▢
ALCOHOL RATING: ●●○○○
STAR RATING: ★★☆☆☆

Shake all of the ingredients together with ice and strain into the glass. To garnish, place a slice of lemon on the rim of the glass and drop in a cherry.

Try adding half a kiwi (sliced) to the ingredients before shaking. The fruit will complement the taste of the gin.

about the Manhattan

Cousin to the Martini, the Manhattan has been a popular cocktail for more than one hundred years. The cocktail is said to have been invented in New York's Manhattan Club at the end of the 19th century for Winston Churchill's American mother.

The Manhattan is a mix of whiskey, sweet vermouth (to temper the drier taste of the whiskey) and bitters (to add a distinctive herbal tang). This cocktail was originally made with straight rye whiskey. However, during the Prohibition years (1920–33), rye whiskey largely disappeared, and once Prohibition had ended American whiskey producers had to begin the whole distillation process from scratch, meaning it was some years until American whiskey was commercially available. On the other hand Canadian whisky (small amounts of which were being smuggled into the US during the 1920s) was immediately available. Thus Canadian whisky became the common base for the Manhattan.

Today, Manhattan drinkers may specify their choice of whiskey to tailor their drink to their individual taste. Try making the Manhattan with straight rye for a more bitter version. Use the comparatively sweet-tasting bourbon if you prefer a sweeter cocktail, or try Canadian whisky for a subtle and balanced mix – Canadian Club is a dry yet smooth brand of Canadian whisky which, in my opinion, works perfectly with the other Manhattan ingredients to make the finest version of this classic drink.

226 **Manhattan**
2 oz / 56 ml whiskey of choice
¼ oz / 7 ml sweet vermouth
2 drops Angostura bitters

GLASS TYPE: Y
ALCOHOL RATING: ●●◐○○
STAR RATING: ★★★★★

Pour the ingredients into a shaker, stir with ice until the shaker is frosted and strain into the glass. Garnish with an orange peel and a cherry.

227 dry manhattan

2 oz / 56 ml whiskey of choice
¾ oz / 21 ml dry vermouth
2 drops Angostura bitters

GLASS TYPE: ▽
ALCOHOL RATING: ●●●○○
STAR RATING: ★★★★★

Pour the ingredients into a shaker, stir with ice until the shaker is frosted
and strain into the glass. Place a lemon peel inside the glass to garnish.
*This is my personal favourite of the manhattan variations – its drier flavour goes
perfectly with a cigar.*

228 perfect manhattan

1 ½ oz / 42 ml whiskey of choice
¼ oz / 7 ml dry vermouth
¼ oz / 7 ml sweet vermouth
2 drops Angostura bitters

GLASS TYPE: ▽
ALCOHOL RATING: ●●○○○
STAR RATING: ★★★☆☆

Pour the ingredients into a shaker, stir with ice until the shaker is frosted,
and strain into the glass. Garnish with an orange peel and a cherry.
*This is the medium-dry version of the Manhattan (see no.226). Try substituting
the bitters with a tablespoon of lemon juice to make a citrus-flavoured manhattan.*

229 Fort William

2 oz / 56 ml blended scotch
juice of 1 lime
¼ tsp grenadine
dash sugar syrup

GLASS TYPE: ▽
ALCOHOL RATING: ●●○○○
STAR RATING: ★★★☆☆

Shake all the ingredients together with ice and strain into the glass. Put a
lemon peel inside the glass to garnish.
*You can make this cocktail more flavoursome by substituting the grenadine
with ¹/₂ tsp of apricot liqueur and ¹/₂ tsp of triple sec. This will also turn the
drink an opaque-orange colour (rather than a deep-red).*

230 Canadian breeze

2 oz / 56 ml Canadian rye whisky
½ tsp maraschino
1 tbsp lemon juice
1 tsp pineapple juice

GLASS TYPE: ▯
ALCOHOL RATING: ●●○○○
STAR RATING: ★★★★☆

Shake all of the ingredients together with ice and strain into an ice-filled
glass. Place a pineapple stick and a cherry inside the glass to garnish.
*In this mix I like to use Canadian Club, which has a hazelnut flavour as it hits
the tongue, followed by a mild citrus aftertaste.*

blue blazer

1 tsp honey
2 oz / 56 ml water (boiling)
2 oz / 56 ml blended scotch

GLASS TYPE: ▯
ALCOHOL RATING: ●●○○○
STAR RATING: ★★★★☆

Using 2 stainless steel mugs with handles, dissolve the honey with the water in 1 mug. Pour the scotch into the other mug and ignite with a match. Then pour the whisky into the first mug. As the whisky burns, pour the mix back and forth from one mug to the other 3 or 4 times to produce a stream of flaming liquid. Once the flame goes out, pour the drink into an old-fashioned glass to serve.

Please exercise extreme caution if you are mixing this drink yourself!

TRADITIONAL CLASSIC

about the blue blazer

This cocktail's name refers to a bright blue flame that streams between two mugs when the whisky is ignited during the mixing of this drink. To turn the Blue Blazer into the ultimate hot toddy; add two cloves, a lemon wheel and a cinnamon stick – perfect on a cold winter's night, and also perfect for relieving the symptoms of colds and 'flu.

Famous bartender Jerry Thomas, whose knack for inventing imaginative and popular cocktails earned him the nickname "Professor", first created this drink in San Francisco more than 150 years ago. The Blue Blazer is rarely made today. To see it will be a true spectacle, but remember to stand well back! If you are attempting to mix this cocktail yourself, wear protective gloves and keep a fire extinguisher handy.

CHAPTER SEVEN

brandy

Brandy was probably invented by Dutch traders in the 16th century. The spirit can be distilled from any kind of fruit, but is most commonly made from grapes. Although brandies are made worldwide, the greatest and most famous come from specific regions of France. The best-known is cognac, from the region around the southwestern French town of Cognac. The spirit's smooth, rounded flavours and high alcohol content make it a popular cocktail base.

Fruit-flavoured brandies also make excellent cocktail ingredients. Although commonly grouped as "brandies", true fruit brandies and fruit brandy liqueurs are different things (see p.15). A true fruit brandy, such as kirsch (a true cherry brandy) in this chapter, is distilled directly from the fruit. A fruit brandy liqueur (such as apricot brandy in this chapter) is made by steeping the fruit in grape spirit. Apple brandy (a true brandy) is distilled directly from apples. The best apple brandies are applejack (produced in the US) and calvados (from Normandy in northern France).

232 apple brandy

1 ½ oz / 42 ml applejack or calvados
1 tsp grenadine
1 tsp lemon juice

GLASS TYPE: ☐
ALCOHOL RATING: ●◐○○○
STAR RATING: ★★★★☆

Shake the ingredients together with ice and strain into the glass. Dangle
a loose apple twist on the rim of the glass to garnish.
*To turn this cocktail into a slow-sipping drink, simply serve it over ice. Fill an
old-fashioned glass with crushed ice and shake and strain the mix into the glass.
Garnish as before.*

233 half moon

2 oz / 56 ml applejack or calvados
dash crème de cassis
juice of 1 lemon
1 tsp powdered (caster) sugar

GLASS TYPE: ☐
ALCOHOL RATING: ●●○○○
STAR RATING: ★★★★☆

Pour all of the ingredients into a shaker, shake with ice and strain into
an ice-filled glass. To garnish, float a slice of apple on top of the ice.
*The crème de cassis adds a hint of sweet blackcurrant to this cocktail. The slice
of apple used as a garnish gives the impression of a crescent moon floating in
a midnight sky – hence the cocktail's name.*

234 special rough

1 ½ oz / 42 ml applejack or calvados
1 ½ oz / 42 ml brandy
½ tsp Pernod

GLASS TYPE: ♀
ALCOHOL RATING: ●●●◐○
STAR RATING: ★★★☆☆

Pre-warm the brandy snifter. Pour the ingredients into a shaker, stir
with ice and strain into the glass.
*To pre-warm a glass see p.20. This mix of liquorice, brandy and apple brandy
creates a harsh, but well-balanced drink.*

235 apple brandy highball

½ Granny Smith apple (peeled, cored and sliced)
2 oz / 56 ml applejack or calvados
ginger ale or soda

GLASS TYPE: ☐
ALCOHOL RATING: ●●○○○
STAR RATING: ★★★☆☆

Muddle the apple in a bowl. Pour the applejack or calvados into a glass filled
with ice. Add the apple. Fill with ginger ale or soda. Place a lemon peel inside
the glass to garnish, and stir.
*The lemon garnish adds a zesty taste to this apple brandy cocktail. If you use ginger
ale, you will sweeten the mix; if you use soda, you will temper the flavours.*

236 A.J.

1 ½ oz / 42 ml applejack or calvados
2 dashes apricot brandy
2 dashes triple sec
1 ½ oz / 42 ml grapefruit juice
dash apple juice

GLASS TYPE: ⧗
ALCOHOL RATING: ●◑○○○
STAR RATING: ★★★☆☆

Shake all the ingredients together with ice and strain into the glass.
Put a slice of apple inside the glass to garnish.
This cocktail also tastes good when made with orange or pineapple juice instead
of the grapefruit juice.

237 apple sour

½ Granny Smith apple (peeled, cored and sliced)
2 oz / 56 ml brandy
1 oz / 28 ml sour mix (see p.17)
1 tsp egg white (optional)

GLASS TYPE: ⧠
ALCOHOL RATING: ●●○○○
STAR RATING: ★★★★☆

Muddle the apple in a shaker. Pour in the remaining ingredients, shake
with ice and strain into an ice-filled glass. Put a slice of lemon, a slice of
apple and a cherry inside the glass to garnish.
The fresh apple adds a tartness to this brandy sour – you may wish to add a dash of
sugar syrup to sweeten. If you shake with egg white (see p.16) you will create
a fluffier cocktail.

238 apple brandy Rickey

1 ½ oz / 42 ml applejack or calvados
2 lime wedges
soda

GLASS TYPE: ⧠
ALCOHOL RATING: ●◑○○○
STAR RATING: ★★☆☆☆

Pour the applejack or calvados into a glass filled with ice. Squeeze the lime
juice into the drink and drop the spent lime into the glass to garnish. Fill with
soda and stir.
This is an apple brandy version of the original Gin Rickey (see no.95). You may
want to add a dash of apple juice to enhance the apple flavour and sweeten this
slow-sipping cocktail.

239 holly blush

¼ Granny Smith apple (peeled, cored and sliced)
2 oz / 56 ml brandy
dash apricot brandy
dash triple sec
juice of ½ lime

GLASS TYPE: ⧗
ALCOHOL RATING: ●●◑○○
STAR RATING: ★★★★★

Muddle the apple in a shaker. Pour in the remaining ingredients, shake
with ice and strain into the glass. Drop in a cherry to garnish.
The combination of red and green ingredients creates a festive-looking drink,
but it tastes great at any time of the year!

brandy mint julep

240

1 peach (peeled and pitted)
2 sprigs mint
1 tsp powdered (caster) sugar
splash water (cold)
2 oz / 56 ml brandy
¼ oz / 7 ml peach schnapps

GLASS TYPE: 🥃
ALCOHOL RATING: ●●○○○
STAR RATING: ★★★★☆

Muddle the peach and mint together with the sugar and water in a highball.
Add the brandy and the peach schnapps and stir. Put 4 thin slices of peach
and 2 mint leaves inside the glass to garnish.

*This cocktail puts a refreshing peach spin on the classic bourbon-based Mint Julep
(see no.194).*

Punch and Judy

241

2 oz / 56 ml brandy
½ oz / 14 ml sweet port
½ oz / 14 ml triple sec
juice of 1 lemon
1 tsp sugar syrup
dash orange juice
lemonade

GLASS TYPE: 🥃
ALCOHOL RATING: ●●●○○
STAR RATING: ★★★★★

Shake all of the ingredients (except for the lemonade) together with ice
and strain into an ice-filled glass. Add a slice of lemon, slice of orange,
2 strawberries and a cinnamon stick. Top with lemonade.

This is a great winter punch.

brandy Alexander

242

1 oz / 28 ml brandy
1 oz / 28 ml crème de cacao (white)
1 oz / 28 ml single cream

GLASS TYPE: 🍸
ALCOHOL RATING: ●●○○○
STAR RATING: ★★★★★

Shake the ingredients with ice and strain into a cocoa-rimmed glass.

*If you're a fan of brandy and can never resist a creamy dessert, this cocktail
is perfect for you – you'll want another and another and …*

brandy Alexander no. 2

243

½ oz / 14 ml brandy
½ oz / 14 ml crème de cacao (brown)
dash Frangelico
½ oz / 14 ml double cream

GLASS TYPE: 🍸
ALCOHOL RATING: ●○○○○
STAR RATING: ★★★★★

Shake all of the ingredients together with ice and strain into the glass.
Place a chocolate wafer straw inside the glass to garnish.

This cocktail is a nutty, less alcoholic version of the Brandy Alexander (see above).

sidecar

1 oz / 28 ml cognac
1 oz / 28 ml Cointreau
juice of ¼ lemon

GLASS TYPE: Y
ALCOHOL RATING: ●●○○○
STAR RATING: ★★★★★

Shake all of the ingredients together with ice and strain into the glass.
Garnish with a lemon wheel.

TRADITIONAL CLASSIC

about the sidecar

The creation of the Sidecar is most commonly attributed to US bartender Harry
MacElhone, founder of the famous Harry's Bar in Paris in 1911 (some sources
say that he created the Sidecar itself in 1923). Traditionally, the cognac,
Cointreau and lemon juice are mixed in the drink in equal quantities to create
a balance of strong, sweet and acidic tastes. More recently, a tendency has
arisen to use two parts cognac to one part each of Cointreau and lemon juice
– but to do this is to upset the perfection of the drink.

Great as an apéritif, the Sidecar should be served ice-cold and be a pale opaque
colour. The flavours should blend so seemlessly into one another that it is
impossible to say, once the strength of the cognac has passed, where the
sweet Cointreau ends and the zesty lemon begins.

245   **B & B**
½ oz / 14 ml Bénédictine
½ oz / 14 ml brandy

GLASS TYPE: ♀
ALCOHOL RATING: ●○○○○
STAR RATING: ★★★★★

Pre-warm a brandy snifter. Pour in the Bénédictine and float the brandy on top.
Pre-warming the glass (see p.20) will help the brandy's aromas to flourish.

246▼   **grape escape**
3 red grapes on a stalk
8 seedless green grapes (plus 5 for garnish)
1 ½ tsp sugar (white, granulated)
2 oz / 56 ml brandy
champagne

GLASS TYPE: ▯
ALCOHOL RATING: ●●○○○
STAR RATING: ★★★★★

Put the red grapes (on their stalk) inside a glass filled with crushed ice.
Muddle the green grapes together with the sugar and brandy in a shaker.
Shake with ice and strain into the prepared glass. Top with champagne.
To garnish, add the remaining 5 green grapes (halved) to the drink.
I created this cocktail for the launch party of the animated movie Chicken Run
(2000). The movie is based on the classic The Great Escape.

247 **brandy twist**
2 oz / 56 ml brandy
2 dashes Angostura bitters
½ tsp sugar syrup

GLASS TYPE: ♀ ♀
ALCOHOL RATING: ●●○○○
STAR RATING: ★★★☆☆

Pour the ingredients into a shaker and stir with ice. Strain into a snifter
filled with 4 or 5 ice cubes. Put a lemon twist inside the glass to garnish.
*You can turn this cocktail into a completely new drink by serving it in a flute
with no ice and topping with champagne. Garnish as before.*

248▼ **brandy collins**
2 oz / 56 ml brandy
juice of ½ lemon
1 tsp powdered (caster) sugar
soda

GLASS TYPE: ▯
ALCOHOL RATING: ●●○○○
STAR RATING: ★★★★★

Shake the first 3 ingredients together with ice and strain into an ice-filled
glass. Top with soda and stir. Garnish with a loose twist of lemon and
a loose twist of lime.
This is the brandy version of the traditional gin-based Tom Collins (see no.57).

249▲ **brandy crusta**
2 oz / 56 ml brandy
½ oz / 14 ml triple sec
dash Angostura bitters
1 tsp maraschino
1 tsp lemon juice

GLASS TYPE: ⅂
ALCOHOL RATING: ●●●○○
STAR RATING: ★★★★☆

Place a tight lemon twist inside a sugar-rimmed glass. Pour all
of the ingredients into a shaker and stir with ice. Strain the mix
into the prepared glass.
*This cocktail is based on the winning combination of triple sec, bitters
and lemon juice.*

250 **black stinger**
2 oz / 56 ml brandy
4 blackberries
2 mint leaves

GLASS TYPE: ⅂
ALCOHOL RATING: ●●○○○
STAR RATING: ★★★★☆

Shake the ingredients with ice. Strain (through a tea strainer) into the glass.
You may wish to add a dash of sugar syrup to sweeten this cocktail.

251   **stirrup cup**
       1 oz / 28 ml brandy
       1 oz / 28 ml cherry brandy
       juice of ½ lemon
       1 tsp sugar syrup

GLASS TYPE: ▢
ALCOHOL RATING: ●●○○○
STAR RATING: ★★☆☆☆

Shake all the ingredients together with ice and strain into an ice-filled glass.
Drop a cherry into the drink to garnish.

This is a bitter and tangy cocktail designed to be sipped slowly.

252▼   **cherry blossom**
       1 ½ oz / 42 ml brandy
       ½ oz / 14 ml cherry brandy
       1 ½ tsp triple sec
       2 tsp lemon juice
       1 ½ tsp grenadine

GLASS TYPE: ▽
ALCOHOL RATING: ●●◐○○
STAR RATING: ★★★★☆

Shake all the ingredients together with ice and strain into a sugar-rimmed
glass. Drop in a cherry to garnish.

Try dipping the rim of the glass in cherry brandy before you rim it with sugar.

253 apricot fizz

1 oz / 28 ml brandy
1 oz / 28 ml apricot brandy
juice of ½ lemon
juice of ½ lime
1 tsp powdered (caster) sugar
soda

GLASS TYPE: ▯
ALCOHOL RATING: ●●○○○
STAR RATING: ★★★★☆

Shake all the ingredients (except for the soda) together with ice and strain into an ice-filled glass. Top with soda. Place 5 slices of fresh apricot inside the glass to garnish.

As an alternative, muddle 2 fresh apricots (pitted) together with the sugar in a shaker. Pour in 2 oz/56 ml regular brandy and add the lemon and lime. Shake, strain, top and garnish as before.

254 royal smile

2 oz / 56 ml brandy
1 tsp apricot brandy
½ oz / 14 ml gin
juice of ¼ lemon
dash sugar syrup
5 fresh raspberries

GLASS TYPE: ▽
ALCOHOL RATING: ●●◐○○
STAR RATING: ★★★★☆

Shake all of the ingredients together with ice and strain into the glass. Place a tight lemon twist inside the glass to garnish.

This brandy and gin mix works well with the sweet apricot and the fresh raspberries.

255 after-dinner cocktail

4 lime wedges
½ oz / 14 ml brandy
½ oz / 14 ml apricot brandy
1 oz / 28 ml triple sec

GLASS TYPE: ▢
ALCOHOL RATING: ●●○○○
STAR RATING: ★★★☆☆

Squeeze the lime wedges over a shaker to release the juice and drop in the spent wedges. Add the remaing ingredients. Shake with ice and pour the mix (including the lime wedges) into the glass.

This cocktail is perfect after a meal – the sour lime will cleanse your palate.

256 apricot special

1 fresh apricot (peeled and pitted)
1 ½ oz / 42 ml brandy
¼ tsp gin
1 tbsp single cream

GLASS TYPE: ▽
ALCOHOL RATING: ●●○○○
STAR RATING: ★★★★★

Muddle the apricot in a shaker. Add the remaining ingredients and shake with ice. Strain the mix into the glass.

The gin adds a hint of juniper flavour to this cocktail.

257 apricot flower

1 fresh apricot (peeled and pitted)
1 ¾ oz / 49 ml brandy
1 ½ tsp apricot brandy
¾ oz / 21 ml sweet vermouth
1 ½ tsp lemon juice

GLASS TYPE: Y
ALCOHOL RATING: ●●○○○
STAR RATING: ★★★★☆

Muddle the apricot in a shaker. Add the remaining ingredients, shake
with ice and strain into the glass. Float an edible flower on the top of
the drink to garnish.
*Try this cocktail with 2 or 3 drops of parfait amour instead of sweet vermouth, to turn
this orange-coloured mix into a purple drink with a floral flavour.*

258 ruby dawn

½ oz / 14 ml brandy
½ oz / 14 ml apricot brandy
½ oz / 14 ml gin
1 oz / 28 ml orange juice
1 tsp grenadine
dash apple juice

GLASS TYPE: ▯
ALCOHOL RATING: ●◐○○○
STAR RATING: ★★★★☆

Shake all of the ingredients together with ice and strain into an ice-filled
glass. To garnish, put 4 or 5 thin slices of apple into the drink.
*This sweet drink reminds me of late nights and early mornings in South Africa –
watching the sun come up over the Indian Ocean. Bliss!*

259 brandied port

1 oz / 28 ml brandy
1 oz / 28 ml port
1 tsp maraschino
juice of ¼ lemon

GLASS TYPE: ▯
ALCOHOL RATING: ●●○○○
STAR RATING: ★★★★☆

Shake all the ingredients together with ice and strain into an ice-filled glass.
Place a slice of orange inside the glass to garnish.
*I prefer to use tawny port. Regular port is bottled-aged, whereas tawny port is
cask-aged for a minimum of 5 years (it can spend 5, 10, 20, 30 or 40 years in casks)
before being bottled, to give it a lighter, slightly sweeter and more complex flavour. I
think this perfectly complements the brandy in this rich-tasting cocktail.*

260 brandy smash

4 sprigs mint
1 sugar cube (white)
2 oz / 56 ml brandy
soda

GLASS TYPE: ▯
ALCOHOL RATING: ●●○○○
STAR RATING: ★★★★★

Muddle the mint together with the sugar in an old-fashioned glass.
Pour in the brandy and add crushed ice. Top with soda and stir.
*A smash is any short drink containing mint, sugar and a spirit, and served
in an old-fashioned glass over crushed ice.*

gimp

1 ½ oz / 42 ml brandy
juice of ½ lemon
½ tsp grenadine

GLASS TYPE: ⑂
ALCOHOL RATING: ●◐○○○
STAR RATING: ★★☆☆☆

Shake the ingredients together with ice and strain into the glass.
This is a simple, sweet-and-sour cocktail.

262▼

brandy daisy

2 oz / 56 ml brandy
juice of ½ lemon
1 tsp raspberry syrup
½ tsp powdered (caster) sugar

GLASS TYPE: ▯
ALCOHOL RATING: ●●○○○
STAR RATING: ★★★★☆

Shake all of the ingredients together with ice and strain into an ice-filled
glass. Garnish with 5 fresh raspberries.
Try this cocktail with fresh raspberries as well as the syrup to enhance the fruit
flavour, and to give the mix a slightly smoother consistency. Muddle 10 raspberries
in a shaker, pour in the listed ingredients. Shake, strain and garnish as before.

263 **brandy cassis**

1 ½ oz / 42 ml brandy
dash crème de cassis
1 oz / 28 ml lemon juice

GLASS TYPE: 🍸
ALCOHOL RATING: ●◐○○○
STAR RATING: ★★★☆☆

Shake all the ingredients together with ice and strain into the glass.
Squeeze a lemon peel over the glass to release the fruit's oils into
the drink, then drop the peel inside the glass to garnish.

This is a sweet, berry-flavoured drink with a citrus tang.

264▾ **widow's kiss**

1 oz / 28 ml brandy
½ oz / 14 ml Bénédictine
½ oz / 14 ml Chartreuse (yellow)
dash Angostura bitters

GLASS TYPE: 🍸
ALCOHOL RATING: ●●●◐○
STAR RATING: ★★☆☆☆

Shake the ingredients with ice and strain into the glass. Garnish
with half a maraschino cherry inside a fresh (stalkless) cherry.

*In this cocktail the strong-tasting, high-proof Chartreuse is disguised by the sweet
herbal-flavoured Bénédictine.*

265 brandy cobbler

1 tsp powdered (caster) sugar
2 oz / 56 ml soda
2 oz / 56 ml brandy

GLASS TYPE: ▢
ALCOHOL RATING: ●●○○○
STAR RATING: ★★★★★

Stir the sugar with the soda in an old-fashioned glass until the sugar
is dissolved. Fill the glass with crushed ice. Add the brandy and stir well.
To garnish, drop 2 blackberries, 2 raspberries and 2 cranberries into
the glass. Serve with straws.
This cocktail is served with straws so that the drinker can use them to crush
the berries – the more they crush, the more berry-flavoured the drink.

266 Gilroy

1 oz / 28 ml brandy
½ oz / 14 ml gin
1 tbsp dry vermouth
dash orange bitters
dash maraschino
juice of ¼ lemon

GLASS TYPE: ♈♀
ALCOHOL RATING: ●●○○○
STAR RATING: ★★☆☆☆

Shake all of the ingredients together with ice and strain into the martini
glass. To garnish, put an orange peel inside the glass and drop in a cherry.
You can also try a warm, stirred version of this cocktail. Pour the ingredients into
a shaker and stir. Serve in a pre-warmed brandy snifter (see p.20).

267 morning glory

2 oz / 56 ml brandy
½ oz / 14 ml dry vermouth
¼ tsp Pernod
¼ tsp triple sec
2 dashes orange bitters
¼ tsp maraschino

GLASS TYPE: ♈
ALCOHOL RATING: ●●●○○
STAR RATING: ★★★☆☆

Pour all of the ingredients into a shaker, stir with ice and strain into
the glass. Drop in a cherry to garnish.
This is a strong, dry drink, with notes of liquorice and bitter orange.

268 pineapple spice

½ cup fresh pineapple (skinned, cored)
juice of ¼ lemon
1 tsp powdered (caster) sugar
2 oz / 56 ml brandy
½ oz / 14 ml triple sec

GLASS TYPE: ♈
ALCOHOL RATING: ●●○○○
STAR RATING: ★★★☆☆

Muddle the pineapple together with the lemon and sugar in a shaker. Add
the brandy and triple sec. Shake with ice and strain into the glass. To
garnish, put a pineapple stick and a cinnamon stick inside the glass.
The cinnamon garnish will temper the sweetness of the pineapple and add a spicy
edge to this drink.

269 grape cooler

7 green seedless grapes (plus 2 for garnish)
3 red seedless grapes (plus 2 for garnish)
½ tsp powdered (caster) sugar
2 oz / 56 ml brandy
2 oz / 56 ml ginger ale

GLASS TYPE: ☐
ALCOHOL RATING: ●●○○○
STAR RATING: ★★★★★

Muddle the green and the red grapes together with the sugar in a shaker.
Pour in the brandy and shake with ice. Strain the mix into an ice-filled glass.
Top with ginger ale and stir. Drop 2 green and 2 red grapes (halved) into the
drink to garnish. Stir again.

*This cocktail is a variation on the Harvard Cooler, which was a popular drink at
Harvard University in the early 1900s. The grapes enhance the flavour of the rich
brandy, and the ginger ale adds a spicy and refreshing taste.*

270 French jam

1 ½ oz / 42 ml brandy
½ oz / 14 ml Jamaica dark rum
½ tsp triple sec
dash Angostura bitters
½ tsp pineapple juice

GLASS TYPE: ♈
ALCOHOL RATING: ●●○○○
STAR RATING: ★★★★☆

Shake all of the ingredients together with ice and strain into the glass.
Put a pineapple stick inside the glass to garnish.

This cocktail makes a fine, pre-dinner tipple.

271 brandy colonial

1 oz / 28 ml brandy
½ oz / 14 ml dry vermouth
½ oz / 14 ml sweet vermouth
½ tsp triple sec
¼ tsp Pernod

GLASS TYPE: ♈
ALCOHOL RATING: ●●●○○
STAR RATING: ★★★☆☆

Shake all of the ingredients together with ice and strain into the glass.
To garnish, put a cucumber stick (including the peel) and a sprig of mint
inside the glass.

The skin should be left on the cucumber garnish, as the skin contains the flavour.

272 saratoga

2 oz / 56 ml brandy
2 dashes Angostura bitters
½ tsp maraschino
1 tsp lemon juice
1 tsp pineapple juice

GLASS TYPE: ♈
ALCOHOL RATING: ●●○○○
STAR RATING: ★★☆☆☆

Shake all of the ingredients together with ice and strain into the glass.
Place a pineapple leaf inside the glass to decorate.

*The dry bitters and the sharp lemon will balance the sweet pineapple
and maraschino, to create a semi-sweet mix.*

liqueurs and
other spirits

Liqueurs (sometimes known as cordials in the US) are sweet, alcoholic drinks made by blending or redistilling a base spirit with a flavouring, or variety of flavourings, and then sweetening. These flavourings are derived from fruits, herbs, spices, barks, berries and flowers.

The origin of liqueurs dates back to the early 16th century, when the drinks were produced for their medicinal qualities and drunk to ward off a variety of ailments. Later, liqueurs became popular apéritifs and digestives – traditionally served neat. It is only fairly recently that they have become common bases for cocktails.

The liqueur-based cocktails in this chapter range from sweet and fruity mixes, such as Sex on the Beach (see no.278), through refreshing drinks, like the Amaretto Sour (see no.302), to rich and creamy after-dinner cocktails, such as Apple Strudel (see no.311). The liqueurs used in this book are listed and described in chapter one (see pp.13–16). Any non-sweet alcoholic bases found in this chapter can be simply defined as an "other spirit".

273 strawberry sunrise

2 oz / 56 ml strawberry liqueur
½ oz / 14 ml grenadine
4 fresh strawberries
orange juice

GLASS TYPE: 🔲
ALCOHOL RATING: ●◑○○○
STAR RATING: ★★★☆☆

Blend the first 3 ingredients together with half a cup of crushed ice until smooth. Pour the mix into the glass and top with orange. Attach one whole strawberry to the rim of the glass to garnish.

This is a refreshing, strawberry variation on the classic Tequila Sunrise (see no.106).

274 mani masi

4 fresh strawberries
1 oz / 28 ml strawberry liqueur
¾ oz / 21 ml vodka
1 oz / 28 ml orange juice
1 oz / 28 ml sour mix (see p.17)

GLASS TYPE: 🔲
ALCOHOL RATING: ●◑○○○
STAR RATING: ★★★☆☆

Muddle the strawberries in a shaker. Pour in the remaining ingredients; shake with ice and strain into a sugar-rimmed, ice-filled glass. Place 3 slices of strawberry inside the glass to garnish.

A fresh strawberry-flavoured cocktail to be drunk on hot summer's days. You can experiment with other fresh fruits and fruit liqueurs, such as melon or raspberry.

275 apple spice

2 oz / 56 ml apple schnapps
splash cinnamon schnapps

GLASS TYPE: 🔲 🔲
ALCOHOL RATING: ●●○○○
STAR RATING: ★★☆☆☆

Pour the ingredients into a glass filled with ice and stir. Place 5 slices of apple and a cinnamon stick inside the glass to garnish.

This drink can also be served as a layered shot: simply pour the apple schnapps into a shot glass and float the cinnamon schnapps on top.

276 crocodile cooler

1 oz / 28 ml Midori
1 oz / 28 ml citrus vodka
¾ oz / 21 ml triple sec
2 oz / 56 ml sour mix (see p.17)
½ oz / 14 ml lime juice
lemonade

GLASS TYPE: 🔲
ALCOHOL RATING: ●●●○○
STAR RATING: ★★★★☆

Pour all of the ingredients (except for the lemonade) into a glass filled with ice. Top with lemonade. To garnish, place a pineapple wedge on the rim of the glass, and a cherry or lime wheel inside the glass.

This cocktail should be a darker colour at the bottom and fainter near the top, like a crocodile lurking beneath the water's surface – watch out for the citrus bite!

Pimm's cup

2 oz / 56 ml Pimm's
¼ oz / 7 ml gin
lemonade and/or ginger ale

GLASS TYPE: ☐
ALCOHOL RATING: ●●○○○
STAR RATING: ★★★★★

Put mint leaves, slices of stawberry, lemon and orange, and a strip of cucumber peel into an ice-filled glass. Pour in the ingredients.

TRADITIONAL CLASSIC

about Pimm's cup

The fruity and refreshing Pimm's Cup is the quintessential English cocktail – the perfect accompaniment to watching a cricket or tennis match under the shade of a tree on a summer's day. However, beware: its pleasant, summery taste masks a pretty strong kick.

The origins of the Pimm's Cup are to be found in Mr James Pimm's Oyster Bar in 19th-century London. Customers would take a glass of the homemade "house cup" with their oysters. Pimm's special blend, based on gin – the spirit of the time – and a variety of fruit extracts and liqueurs, soon became widely popular. As a result the Pimm's company began to market the drink commercially. To this day the precise recipe remains a secret. Pimm's also make a vodka version of their drink, which you may like to try as an alternative in your Pimm's Cup.

sex on the beach

1 oz / 28 ml peach schnapps
¾ oz / 21 ml vodka
cranberry juice
orange juice

GLASS TYPE: ▯
ALCOHOL RATING: ●●○○○
STAR RATING: ★★★★☆

Pour the peach schnapps and the vodka into a sugar-rimmed glass filled with ice. Top with cranberry and orange. Garnish with an orange wheel and a wedge of lime.

MODERN CLASSIC

about sex on the beach

A popular classic, this frequently ordered cocktail is a true product of its time, with a name and ingredients to match. Bartenders found that the sweet, fruity liqueur mixed well with orange which, in turn, mixed well with cranberry. They added a shot of vodka to perk it up, gave it a suitably youthful and hedonistic title, and Sex on the Beach was born.

The sweet and palatable peach schnapps is not technically a schnapps, but a liqueur, and bears no resemblance to the schnapps traditionally drunk in Scandinavia, which is a strong and dry clear spirit or liqueur made from grain or potato. However, the term schnapps was borrowed to help remarket liqueurs for a young audience in the late 1980s. The rebranding was a success and peach schnapps soon became one of the most fashionable drinks around.

279 twin peach

2 oz / 56 ml peach schnapps
4 oz / 112 ml cranberry juice
2 oz / 56 ml lychee syrup (tinned)

GLASS TYPE: ▯
ALCOHOL RATING: ●◑○○○
STAR RATING: ★★★☆☆

Shake the ingredients together with ice and strain into an ice-filled glass.
Stir. Put 2 slices of peach and 2 lychees (tinned) inside the glass to garnish.
You can turn this sweet afternoon cocktail into a longer, sparkling drink by adding
a dash of lemonade.

280 fuzzy navel

1 oz / 28 ml peach schnapps
¾ oz / 21 ml vodka
orange juice
dash soda

GLASS TYPE: ▯
ALCOHOL RATING: ●◑○○○
STAR RATING: ★★★☆☆

Pour the first 2 ingredients into a glass filled with ice and stir. Top with
orange juice, leaving just enough room to add the soda. Finally, place a slice
of orange inside the glass to garnish.
This is a fizzy variation on the classic Sex on the Beach (see opposite), and is the
ultimate recipe for cocktail virgins – easy to make and even easier to drink.

281 snow cap

1 ½ oz / 42 ml peach schanpps
4 oz / 112 ml pineapple juice
dash sour mix (see p.17)
soda

GLASS TYPE: ▯
ALCOHOL RATING: ●◑○○○
STAR RATING: ★★★☆☆

Shake the first 3 ingredients together with ice and strain into an ice-filled
glass. Top with soda. Attach a wedge of peach and a wedge of pineapple to
the rim of the glass to decorate.
This sweet and refreshing cocktail gets its name from the soda top, which gives the
drink a snow-capped look.

282 something breezy

1 oz / 28 ml amaretto
1 oz / 28 ml peach schnapps
2 oz / 56 ml cranberry juice
2 oz / 56 ml pineapple juice

GLASS TYPE: ▯
ALCOHOL RATING: ●●○○○
STAR RATING: ★★★☆☆

Shake all the ingredients together with ice and pour into an ice-filled glass.
To garnish, drop a wedge of lime and 3 cranberries into the drink. Serve
with a straw.
You can crush the cranberries with the straw to enhance the berry flavour of
this cocktail.

283 French Canadian

½ oz / 14 ml amaretto
½ oz / 14 ml Chambord
½ oz / 14 ml vodka
½ oz / 14 ml cranberry juice

GLASS TYPE: Y
ALCOHOL RATING: ●◐○○○
STAR RATING: ★★☆☆☆

Shake all of the ingredients together with ice and strain into the glass.
Put 3 fresh cranberries into the drink to garnish.

*This drink was created in the late 1990s by UK bartender Chris Maxwell. The mix of
amaretto and Chambord creates a balanced, berry-flavoured, sweet martini.*

284▼ French fantasy

1 oz / 28 ml Chambord
1 oz / 28 ml triple sec
2 oz / 56 ml cranberry juice
2 oz / 56 ml orange juice

GLASS TYPE: ☐
ALCOHOL RATING: ●●○○○
STAR RATING: ★★★★☆

Pour the ingredients into a glass filled with ice and stir. Garnish with a slice
of orange and a fresh cherry.

In this cocktail you will taste the raspberry and cranberry as two distinct flavours.

285▲ ## melon cooler

1 slice fresh honeydew melon (without rind)
1 oz / 28 ml Midori
½ oz / 14 ml crème de framboise
½ oz / 14 ml peach schnapps
2 oz / 56 ml pineapple juice

GLASS TYPE: ▽
ALCOHOL RATING: ●●○○○
STAR RATING: ★★★★☆

Muddle the melon in a shaker. Pour in the remaining ingredients, shake
with ice and strain into the glass. Decorate with a lime wheel and a cherry.
This is a delicious melon-flavoured summer drink.

286 ## sheer elegance

1 ½ oz / 42 ml amaretto
1 ½ oz / 42 ml crème de framboise
½ oz / 14 ml vodka

GLASS TYPE: ▽
ALCOHOL RATING: ●●●○○
STAR RATING: ★★★☆☆

Shake the ingredients together with ice and strain into the glass. Drop
in 2 raspberries to garnish.
You can dilute this strong drink by shaking the mix for a little longer.

287 blackthorn

1 ½ oz / 42 ml sloe gin
1 oz / 28 ml sweet vermouth

GLASS TYPE: ⍦ ▯
ALCOHOL RATING: ●●◐○○
STAR RATING: ★★☆☆☆

Shake the ingredients together with ice and strain into the glass. Place
a lemon peel inside the glass to garnish.
*Sloe gin, although often thought of as a type of gin, is a liqueur – made by steeping
sloe berries in gin (see p.16). It is red-brown in colour. You can also serve this
cocktail as a long drink: add a dash of sugar syrup before you shake, then strain
into a highball filled with ice and top with soda. Garnish as before.*

288 sloe 'Sisco Bay

¾ oz / 21 ml sloe gin
¾ oz / 21 ml dry vermouth
¾ oz / 21 ml sweet vermouth
dash Angostura bitters
dash orange bitters

GLASS TYPE: ⍦
ALCOHOL RATING: ●●◐○○
STAR RATING: ★★★☆☆

Shake all of the ingredients together with ice and strain into the glass.
Drop in a cherry to garnish.
*This refined mix of dry and sweet vermouth is a sloe gin version of the classic
whiskey Manhattan (see no.226).*

289 orange squeezer

1 ½ oz / 42 ml sloe gin
¾ oz / 21 ml triple sec
dash orange bitters

GLASS TYPE: ⍦
ALCOHOL RATING: ●●◐○○
STAR RATING: ★★★☆☆

Shake the ingredients together with ice and strain into the glass. Squeeze
an orange peel over the drink then drop the peel inside the glass to garnish.
*Squeezing the orange peel over the drink will release the fruit's oils into the drink,
adding a citrus tang to this cocktail.*

290 sloe vanilla

1 ½ oz / 42 ml sloe gin
¾ oz / 21 ml triple sec
1 tsp Pernod

GLASS TYPE: ▯
ALCOHOL RATING: ●●◐○○
STAR RATING: ★★★☆☆

Shake the ingredients together with ice and strain into the glass.
To garnish, put 5 thin strips of vanilla inside the glass.
*The vanilla strips (garnish) give the drink an immediate aroma of vanilla, while their
flavour is gradually released into the mix.*

291 **sloe gin Rickey**
2 oz / 56 ml sloe gin
juice of ½ lime
soda

GLASS TYPE: ⬚
ALCOHOL RATING: ●●○○○
STAR RATING: ★★★☆☆

Pour the sloe gin and the lime into a glass filled with ice and stir. Top
with soda. Place a loose twist of lime inside the glass to garnish.
*This is the sloe berry version of the original Gin Rickey (see no.95). You may wish
to add a dash of sugar syrup to taste.*

292 **sloe vermouth**
1 oz / 28 ml sloe gin
¾ oz / 21 ml dry vermouth
1 tbsp lemon juice

GLASS TYPE: Y
ALCOHOL RATING: ●●○○○
STAR RATING: ★★☆☆☆

Pour the ingredients into a shaker, stir with ice and strain into the glass.
This is a dry, berry-flavoured martini, with a slight citrus tang.

293 **Moulin Rouge**
1 ½ oz / 42 ml sloe gin
¾ oz / 21 ml sweet vermouth
dash Angostura bitters

GLASS TYPE: Y
ALCOHOL RATING: ●●○○○
STAR RATING: ★★★★☆

Pour the ingredients into a shaker. Stir with ice until the shaker is frosted
and strain into the glass. Place a lemon twist inside the glass to garnish.
*Stirring the ingredients with ice until the shaker is frosted will dilute the drink
to make an easier-to-drink cocktail.*

294 **sloe orange**
2 oz / 56 ml sloe gin
¼ tsp dry vermouth
dash orange bitters

GLASS TYPE: Y
ALCOHOL RATING: ●●○○○
STAR RATING: ★★★☆☆

Pour the ingredients into a shaker. Stir with ice until the shaker is frosted
(to chill the gin) and strain into the glass. Squeeze an orange peel over
the drink and drop the spent peel inside the glass to garnish.
The oil from the orange peel will enhance the orange flavour of the bitters.

295 Americano

1 oz / 28 ml Campari
1 oz / 28 ml sweet vermouth
soda

GLASS TYPE: ▯
ALCOHOL RATING: ●●●○○○
STAR RATING: ★★★☆☆

Pour the Campari and the vermouth into a glass filled with ice. Top
with soda and stir. Place a slice of orange inside the glass to garnish.
This is a refreshing mix, based on the famous herbal Italian apéritif Campari. Try the
classic Negroni (see no.72), which is the gin version of this cocktail, too.

296 cherry choc

¾ oz / 21 ml crème de cacao (white)
¾ oz / 21 ml dry vermouth
dash Angostura bitters
½ oz / 14 ml maraschino

GLASS TYPE: ▽
ALCOHOL RATING: ●●○○○○
STAR RATING: ★★☆☆☆

Pour all the ingredients into a shaker, stir with ice and strain into the glass.
Dangle a pair of fresh cherries over the rim of the glass to decorate.
The vermouth and the bitters break down the sweetness of the liqueur
and the maraschino to form a more refined, pre-dinner cocktail.

297 speedy retto

1 oz / 28 ml amaretto
1 oz / 28 ml dry vermouth
½ oz / 14 ml sour mix (see p.17)
soda

GLASS TYPE: ▯
ALCOHOL RATING: ●●○○○
STAR RATING: ★★☆☆☆

Pour the first 3 ingredients into a glass filled with ice. Top with soda
and put a tight lemon twist inside the glass to garnish.
This is a light and refreshing after-dinner cocktail.

298 yellow parrot

¾ oz / 21 ml Chartreuse (yellow)
¾ oz / 21 ml apricot brandy
½ oz / 14 ml Galliano
1 tsp Pernod

GLASS TYPE: ▽▯
ALCOHOL RATING: ●●●◐○
STAR RATING: ★★☆☆☆

Shake all the ingredients together with ice and strain into the glass.
This is a strong, herbal-tasting cocktail. To temper the alcohol, serve this drink
in an old-fashioned glass filled with ice.

LIQUEURS AND OTHER SPIRITS

299 ▲ St Patrick's Day

¾ oz / 21 ml crème de menthe (green)
¾ oz / 21 ml Chartreuse (green)
¾ oz / 21 ml Irish whiskey
dash Angostura bitters

GLASS TYPE: ▼
ALCOHOL RATING: ●●●◐○
STAR RATING: ★★☆☆☆

Pour the ingredients into a shaker, stir with ice and strain into the glass.

Alternatively, you can flame this drink to create a more potent cocktail. Pour all the ingredients (except for the Chartreuse) into a shaker, stir and strain as before. Float the Chartreuse on top, then ignite the top of the drink using a lighter or a match. Please take care when setting drinks alight!

300 kir

¼ oz / 7 ml crème de cassis
dry white wine

GLASS TYPE: ▽
ALCOHOL RATING: ●○○○○
STAR RATING: ★★★★☆

Pour the cassis into the glass and top with wine.
A clean-tasting pre-dinner cocktail, this mix is also popular with champagne instead of wine, in which case it is called a Kir Royale (see no.344).

301 Italian surfer

1 oz / 28 ml amaretto
1 oz / 28 ml brandy
pineapple juice

GLASS TYPE: 🥃
ALCOHOL RATING: ●●○○○
STAR RATING: ★★☆☆☆

Pour the amaretto and the brandy into an ice-filled glass. Fill with pineapple juice and put a pineapple wedge inside the glass to garnish.

The pineapple makes this cocktail a great thirst-quencher. The drink is said to be a popular choice for the competitors after a surfing competition – hence the name!

302▼ amaretto sour

2 oz / 56 ml amaretto
¾ oz / 21 ml lemon juice
dash sugar syrup
1 tsp egg white (optional)

GLASS TYPE: 🥃
ALCOHOL RATING: ●●○○○
STAR RATING: ★★★★☆

Shake all the ingredients together with ice and strain into an ice-filled glass. Garnish with a slice of orange.

This is dedicated to Taz – you're the only one who loved the way I made this drink. Shaking with egg white is optional (see p.16).

303 **boccie ball**

1 ½ oz / 42 ml amaretto
1 ½ oz / 42 ml orange juice
2 oz / 56 ml soda

GLASS TYPE: ▯
ALCOHOL RATING: ●◐○○○
STAR RATING: ★★★☆☆

Pour the amaretto and the orange into a glass filled with ice. Top with soda and put an orange slice inside the glass to garnish.

This refreshing summer-time mix tastes of almond, apricot and orange.

304 **amaretto lime**

1 ½ oz / 42 ml amaretto
½ oz / 14 ml lime cordial
soda

GLASS TYPE: ▯
ALCOHOL RATING: ●◐○○○
STAR RATING: ★★★☆☆

Pour the amaretto and lime cordial into a glass filled with ice. Fill with soda.

The lime and the soda will temper the sweetness of the amaretto to create an easier-to-drink, lime alternative to the Amaretto Sour (see opposite).

305 **thunder and lightning**

½ oz / 14 ml parfait amour
½ oz / 14 ml blue curaçao
½ oz / 14 ml amaretto
¾ oz / 21 ml vodka
2 oz / 56 ml sour mix (see p.17)
1 oz / 28 ml soda

GLASS TYPE: ▯
ALCOHOL RATING: ●●◐○○
STAR RATING: ★★★☆☆

Place a loose twist of lime and a loose twist of orange inside a glass, then fill the glass with ice. Layer the drink by carefully pouring the ingredients, in order, into the prepared glass.

This cocktail takes its name from its garnish – the idea is that the loose twists will create the effect of streaks of lightning inside the glass.

306 **amore-Ade**

1 ¼ oz / 35 ml amaretto
¾ oz / 21 ml triple sec
3 oz / 84 ml soda

GLASS TYPE: 🍷
ALCOHOL RATING: ●●○○○
STAR RATING: ★★★☆☆

Pour the ingredients into a large wine glass and add ice. Put a loose twist of orange inside the glass to garnish.

The soda makes this sweet, citrus cocktail an easy-to-drink mix – just right for summer afternoons.

307   French connection

¾ oz / 21 ml amaretto
1 ½ oz / 42 ml brandy

GLASS TYPE: ♀
ALCOHOL RATING: ●●◔○○
STAR RATING: ★★★☆☆

Pour the amaretto and the brandy into an ice-filled glass and stir.
This is a rich, predominantly amaretto-flavoured cocktail.

308▾   road runner

½ oz / 14 ml amaretto
1 oz / 28 ml vodka
1 oz / 28 ml coconut milk

GLASS TYPE: ♀
ALCOHOL RATING: ●●○○○
STAR RATING: ★★★★☆

Blend the ingredients together with half a cup of crushed ice until smooth.
To garnish, rub the rim of the glass with an orange peel, until moist, then dip
the rim in a sugar and nutmeg mixture. Pour the mix into the prepared glass
and sprinkle a little nutmeg on top of the drink.
Although vodka provides the base for this drink, the amaretto gives it its flavour.

lover's kiss

½ oz / 14 ml amaretto
½ oz / 14 ml cherry brandy
½ oz / 14 ml crème de cacao (brown)
1 oz / 28 ml single cream

GLASS TYPE: ▯
ALCOHOL RATING: ●◑○○○
STAR RATING: ★★★★☆

Shake all the ingredients with ice and strain into an ice-filled glass.
To decorate use sprinkles of cocoa powder and drop a cherry into the drink.
This drink is also served well with strawberry syrup and whipped cream, which turns
it into a sundae cocktail.

hazel cream

1 oz / 28 ml Frangelico
1 oz / 28 ml Kalúha
¾ oz / 21 ml vodka
splash milk or single cream

GLASS TYPE: ▯
ALCOHOL RATING: ●●◑○○
STAR RATING: ★★★★★

Pour all the ingredients into a glass filled with ice. Sprinkle coffee
granules (pictured) or crushed hazelnuts on top of the drink to garnish.
The hazelnut and coffee work beautifully together to create a rich after-dinner drink.

311▲ **apple strudel**
½ oz / 14 ml apple brandy
½ oz / 14 ml light rum
½ oz / 14 ml sweet vermouth
dash apricot brandy
1 tsp lemon juice
dash grenadine
dash single cream

GLASS TYPE: 🍸
ALCOHOL RATING: ●●○○○
STAR RATING: ★★★★☆

Shake all of the ingredients together with ice and strain into the glass.
Garnish with 2 cinnamon sticks and a sprinkle of cinnamon.

This cocktail tastes like a dessert: spicy apples with cream – delicious!

golden cadillac

312

2 oz / 56 ml crème de cacao (white)
1 oz / 28 ml Galliano
1 oz / 28 ml single cream

GLASS TYPE: ♀
ALCOHOL RATING: ●●●○○
STAR RATING: ★★★★★

Blend all of the ingredients together until smooth and pour into the glass.
*Galliano is a sweet and spicy Italian liqueur, which is named after the general
Giuseppe Galliano for his heroic defence of Fort Edna in the Italian-Abyssinian
war of 1896.*

golden dream

313

1 oz / 28 ml Galliano
½ oz / 14 ml triple sec
¼ oz / 7 ml vanilla vodka
1 tbsp orange juice
1 tbsp single cream

GLASS TYPE: ▽
ALCOHOL RATING: ●◑○○○
STAR RATING: ★★★☆☆

Shake all the ingredients vigorously with ice and strain into the glass.
Place 6 thin strips of orange peel inside the glass to garnish.

*This mix of oranges and cream, with a hint of vanilla, makes a perfect after-dinner
cocktail. You can use regular vodka and vanilla extract instead of vanilla vodka.*

Don Pedro

314

½ oz / 14 ml Kalúha
½ oz / 14 ml light rum
5 scoops vanilla ice cream

GLASS TYPE: ♀
ALCOHOL RATING: ●○○○○
STAR RATING: ★★★★★

Pour the ingredients into a shaker and stir until smooth. Pour the mix into
a brandy snifter. To garnish, sprinkle unsalted nuts of your choice on top
of the drink.
*You can try this cocktail with any flavoured liqueur that you fancy instead of
the Kalúha.*

grasshopper

315

equal parts:
crème de menthe (green)
crème de menthe (white)
single cream

GLASS TYPE: ▯ ▽
ALCOHOL RATING: ●●○○○
STAR RATING: ★★☆☆☆

Layer the drink by pouring the ingredients, in order, into a shot glass.
*Some people prefer this famous drink served as a martini. Use ¾ oz/21 ml of each
ingredient. Shake with ice and strain into a martini glass.*

bushwacker

316

½ oz / 14 ml amaretto
½ oz / 14 ml Baileys
½ oz / 14 ml Kalúha
½ oz / 14 ml light rum
2 oz / 56 ml single cream

GLASS TYPE: ▢
ALCOHOL RATING: ●◑○○○
STAR RATING: ★★★★☆

Blend all the ingredients together with half a cup of crushed ice and pour into the glass. Garnish with a sprinkle of cocoa powder.
This is an extremely richly-flavoured and creamy after-dinner cocktail.

peach berry

317

1 oz / 28 ml peach schnapps
½ oz / 14 ml crème de framboise
3 oz / 84 ml single cream

GLASS TYPE: ▢
ALCOHOL RATING: ●◑○○○
STAR RATING: ★★★★☆

Shake the ingredients vigorously with ice and pour into an ice-filled glass. To garnish, place 3 slices of peach inside the glass and put 1 whole raspberry on top of the ice.
You can really taste the fruity flavours in this creamy cocktail.

chocolate strawberry

318

1 oz / 28 ml strawberry liqueur
½ oz / 14 ml crème de cacao (white)
½ oz / 14 ml single cream

GLASS TYPE: ▽
ALCOHOL RATING: ●●○○○
STAR RATING: ★★★☆☆

Pour all the ingredients into a shaker, shake and strain into a large wine glass filled with ice. To garnish, place a fresh strawberry inside the glass and sprinkle chocolate flakes on top of the drink.
The unbeatable combination of strawberry, chocolate and cream makes this cocktail a delicious after-dinner treat – who could resist?

raspberry cream

319

¾ oz / 21 ml Kalúha
¾ oz / 21 ml crème de framboise
1 oz / 28 ml Baileys
soda

GLASS TYPE: ▢
ALCOHOL RATING: ●●◑○○
STAR RATING: ★★☆☆☆

Pour the first 3 ingredients, in order, into a glass filled with ice. Fill with soda and stir. Drop 2 fresh raspberries into the drink to garnish.
Not many cocktails mix cream with soda beacause the cream will usually separate. However, in this cocktail the liqueurs act as combining agents.

320 **peppermint cream**
1 ½ oz / 42 ml crème de cacao (white)
1 oz / 28 ml crème de menthe (white)
1 oz / 28 ml single cream

GLASS TYPE: Y
ALCOHOL RATING: ●●◐○○
STAR RATING: ★★★☆☆

Shake the ingredients together with ice and strain into the glass. Sprinkle cocoa powder on top of the drink to garnish.

When it comes to after-dinner cocktails, mint and cream are a winning combination. Try the ice cream version (see below) for a dessert substitute.

321▼ **peppermint twist**
1 ½ oz / 42 ml crème de menthe (white)
½ oz / 14 ml crème de cacao (white)
3 scoops vanilla ice cream

GLASS TYPE: ♈
ALCOHOL RATING: ●●○○○
STAR RATING: ★★★★★

Blend the ingredients together with half a cup of ice until smooth. Pour the mix into the glass. To garnish, crush a chocolate-covered peppermint candy stick and sprinkle on top of the drink.

This minty cocktail is a dessert in itself. Serve with a straw if you like – but place it to the side rather than in the cocktail so as not to spoil your garnish.

322 B-52

equal parts:
Kalúha
Baileys
Grand Marnier

GLASS TYPE: ▯
ALCOHOL RATING: ●●○○○
STAR RATING: ★★★★☆

Layer the drink by pouring the ingredients, in order, into a shot glass.
This is the original way to make a B-52. However, you can replace the Grand Marnier with double cream, or a light liqueur, such as peppermint, if you wish.

323 blackjack

½ oz / 14 ml black sambuca
½ oz / 14 ml brandy
an espresso (hot)

GLASS TYPE: ▯
ALCOHOL RATING: ●●○○○
STAR RATING: ★★☆☆☆

Shake the ingredients together with ice and strain into an ice-filled glass.
Sambuca is a liquorice-flavoured liqueur, produced by infusing alcohol with elderberries and anise. The ice will temper the strong-tasting alcohol. Try this cocktail with a dash of cream to give a smoother and sweeter finish.

324 toasted almond

1 ½ oz / 42 ml Kalúha
1 oz / 28 ml amaretto
1 ½ oz / 42 ml milk

GLASS TYPE: ▯ Y
ALCOHOL RATING: ●●●○○
STAR RATING: ★★★★★

Pour the ingredients into a glass filled with ice and stir. Sprinkle toasted almonds (crushed) on top of the drink to garnish.
To create a smoother and richer-tasting version of this drink, use single cream instead of milk. Shake with ice and strain into a martini glass. Garnish as before.

325 mint iced coffee

1 oz / 28 ml crème de cacao (white)
1 oz / 28 ml crème de menthe (white)
¾ oz / 21 ml brandy
a triple espresso (cooled)

GLASS TYPE: ▯
ALCOHOL RATING: ●●●○○
STAR RATING: ★★★☆☆

Shake all of the ingredients together with ice and pour into the glass. Stir. Place a tight lemon twist inside the glass to garnish.
If you like iced coffee, you'll love this cocktail. You may also want to try this drink with hot coffee and a float of cream (see Irish Coffee; no.218).

absinthe special

1 ½ oz / 42 ml absinthe
1 tsp powdered (caster) sugar
1 oz / 28 ml water (cold)

GLASS TYPE: ▯
ALCOHOL RATING: ●●●●●
STAR RATING: ★★★★★

Pour the absinthe into the glass. Place the sugar on a bar spoon and dip the spoon into the glass to soak the sugar with absinthe. Take the spoon out and hold it over the glass. Set light to the sugar. Burn the sugar until it starts bubbling and begins to caramelize. Place the spoon inside the glass and stir the burning sugar together with the absinthe. While stirring, slowly pour in the water until the flame goes out. Serve. Beware: the glass will be hot!

TRADITIONAL CLASSIC

about the absinthe special

Absinthe was first created in 1792 by a French physician, Dr Ordinaire. His recipe involved the masceration of woodworm and herbs and spices, such as camomile, aniseed and liquorice, in neutral alcohol. Nicknamed the "green fairy", absinthe grew popular among the Parisian café-goers. However, by the late 1800s, the drink had gained a bad reputation – absinthe was blamed for violence-inducing hallucinations, and was even said to have been instrumental in Van Gogh's infamous ear-cutting incident. Absinthe was banned in most countries in the early 20th century, and remains illegal in the US and much of Europe today, where Herbsaint and Pernod are common substitutes for it. If you happen to be drinking in a country where absinthe is legal (such as the UK and Canada), you must try an Absinthe Special at least once in your life.

327 Vya fashion

1 sugar cube (white)
2 drops Angostura bitters
1 orange peel
1 oz / 28 ml Vya extra-dry vermouth
1 oz / 28 ml Vya sweet vermouth

GLASS TYPE: ▢
ALCOHOL RATING: ●●○○○
STAR RATING: ★★★★★

Place the sugar cube in an old-fashioned glass and pour the bitters
onto the cube, to soak it in bitters. Add the orange peel and a dash each
of extra-dry and sweet Vya vermouth. Muddle the ingredients. Stir the mix
and as you do so slowly pour in the remaining vermouth. Continue to stir and
add ice until the glass is frosted and filled with ice.

*This is a Vya vermouth version of the Old-fashioned (see no.211). Vya is a fruity and
delicate Californian vermouth, currently highly popular in the US. This mix is the most
recent addition to my cocktail list.*

328 rocky mezzanine

1 tbsp maraschino
½ oz / 14 ml brandy
½ oz / 14 ml triple sec
½ oz / 14 ml light rum

GLASS TYPE: ▢
ALCOHOL RATING: ●●●○○
STAR RATING: ★★☆☆☆

Layer the drink by pouring the ingredients, in order, into a glass filled
with ice.

*The ice breaks down the strength of this high-proof cocktail, which owes its name to
the tier effect – created by layering the alcohol.*

329 heat wave

1 ¼ oz / 35 ml coconut liqueur
½ oz / 14 ml peach schnapps
½ oz / 14 ml apricot brandy
3 oz / 84 ml orange juice
3 oz / 84 ml pineapple juice

GLASS TYPE: ▯
ALCOHOL RATING: ●●○○○
STAR RATING: ★★★★☆

Shake all the ingredients together with ice and strain into an ice-filled glass.
Put a slice of fresh peach inside the glass to garnish.

This is a sweet, exotic, golden-coloured cocktail.

330 forest flower

1 oz / 28 ml parfait amour
1 tbsp crème de cacao (white)
1 tbsp single cream
1 tsp grenadine

GLASS TYPE: ▽
ALCOHOL RATING: ●●○○○
STAR RATING: ★★★☆☆

Shake all the ingredients together with ice and strain into the glass. Garnish
with an edible flower, such as a violet or nasturtium.

Parfait amour tastes of violets and lavender; hence this cocktail's name.

331 goober

1 ½ oz / 42 ml crème de framboise
1 ½ oz / 42 ml Midori
1 oz / 28 ml triple sec
1 oz / 28 ml vodka
4 oz / 112 ml orange juice
3 oz / 84 ml pineapple juice
1 oz / 28 ml grenadine

GLASS TYPE: ▯
ALCOHOL RATING: ●●●●○
STAR RATING: ★★★★☆

Pour all of the ingredients into a shaker. Shake with ice and strain into an ice-filled glass. Put 2 slices of kiwi and 2 fresh raspberries inside the glass to garnish.

This is an outstanding, fruity mix. Adding vodka to a liqueur-based cocktail will immediately lessen the sweetness and enhance the alcohol content of the drink.

332 splash and crash

2 oz / 56 ml amaretto
6 oz / 168 ml cranberry juice
2 oz / 56 ml orange juice
½ oz / 14 ml 151-proof rum

GLASS TYPE: ▯
ALCOHOL RATING: ●●●○○
STAR RATING: ★★★★☆

Pour the first 3 ingredients into a glass filled with ice. Float the rum on top. To garnish, place a lime wheel inside the drink and drop in 3 cranberries. Serve with a straw.

This drink is unstirred and should be drunk through a straw. The idea is that, once you reach the end of the drink, the 151 proof rum will really hit you!

333 sweet señorita

1 oz / 28 ml port
¾ oz / 21 ml brandy
¼ tsp triple sec
¾ oz / 21 ml pineapple juice
¼ tsp grenadine

GLASS TYPE: ▽
ALCOHOL RATING: ●●○○○
STAR RATING: ★★☆☆☆

Shake all the ingredients together with ice and strain into a glass. Place a cinnamon stick inside the glass to garnish.

This is a variation of the Spanish summer drink sangria. This mix is made with port instead of red wine for a stronger, more full-bodied cocktail.

334 rusty nail

1 oz / 28 ml Drambuie
1 oz / 28 ml blended scotch

GLASS TYPE: ▯
ALCOHOL RATING: ●●○○○
STAR RATING: ★★★★☆

Pour the ingredients into a glass filled with ice and stir.

Drambuie is made of blended scotch whisky and heather honey (from bees feeding on heather flowers). This is a smooth and simple drink – popular in cigar bars.

champagne

Champagne takes its name from a small district in northeastern France, around the towns of Rheims and Epernay, where it is made. The cooler climate and shorter growing season of this region hasten the harvesting of grapes. Thus, the fermentation process takes place when the grapes are only partially ripe. Acidic, partially ripened grapes are ideal for making sparkling wine. Champagne was originally made by hand-picking the grapes and then pressing them gently and quickly, to avoid the possibility of oxidation. The grape juices began to ferment, as a still wine, until the autumn chill would halt the process. In early spring the partly fermented wine was bottled, and yeast and sugar added. As the weather warmed up, a second fermentation occurred inside the bottle, to create the famous bubbles. Modern methods are more controlled, but essentially follow the same process.

When mixing champagne cocktails, always add the champagne last – to maintain the fizz. Pour slowly, to prevent the bubbles exploding over the top of the glass. Never add champagne to a shaker, or you will risk the mix exploding!

335 **Bellini**

1 oz / 28 ml peach purée
dash peach schnapps
champagne

GLASS TYPE: 🍸
ALCOHOL RATING: ●●○○○
STAR RATING: ★★★☆☆

Pour the purée and the liqueur into a flute and top with champagne. Garnish with a twisted peel of peach.

Invented at Harry's Bar, Venice, in the 1940s, this cocktail is said to be named after the 15th-century painter Giovanni Bellini, owing to the use of glowing pinks in his paintings.

336 **nikiski bellini**

1 oz / 28 ml vodka
dash peach schnapps
2 oz / 56 ml peach purée
champagne

GLASS TYPE: 🍸
ALCOHOL RATING: ●●◐○○
STAR RATING: ★★★★☆

Shake the first 3 ingredients together with ice and pour the mix into the flute. Top with champagne and drop 4 peach slices into the flute to garnish.

Be careful when drinking this cocktail: the vodka will enhance the alcohol volume, but the taste of the vodka will be overpowered by the champagne and peach – the drink will taste less alcoholic than it is.

337 **strawberry bellini**

1 ½ oz / 42 ml gin
dash strawberry liqueur
1 oz / 28 ml strawberry purée
champagne

GLASS TYPE: 🍸
ALCOHOL RATING: ●●◐○○
STAR RATING: ★★★★★

Pour the first 3 ingredients into a flute and stir. Top with champagne (pouring slowly) and stir again. Place one whole strawberry on the rim of the flute to garnish.

This is a delicious example of how to mix strawberries and champagne, and should be drunk while watching a tennis match! This drink also tastes good with raspberry liqueur instead of strawberry. For a spicy alternative, try adding 3 thin strips of fresh ginger before you stir the mix.

338 **gin-schnapp**

1 oz / 28 ml peach schnapps
½ oz / 14 ml gin
1 oz / 28 ml orange juice
champagne

GLASS TYPE: 🍸
ALCOHOL RATING: ●●○○○
STAR RATING: ★★★☆☆

Pour the first 3 ingredients into a flute and stir. Top with champagne. Put a slice of peach inside the flute to garnish.

This is a sweet yet refreshing and easy-to-drink cocktail – great for late-afternoons.

339▲ **mimo-sec**

1 oz / 28 ml triple sec
champagne

GLASS TYPE: 🍸
ALCOHOL RATING: ●●○○○
STAR RATING: ★★★★☆

Pour the triple sec into a flute and top with champagne. Garnish with a loose orange twist.

This cocktail is based on the Mimosa (see below) – made with triple sec rather than orange juice.

340 **mimosa**

1 oz / 28 ml orange juice
dash Grand Marnier
champagne

GLASS TYPE: 🍸
ALCOHOL RATING: ●○○○○
STAR RATING: ★★★★☆

Pour the orange juice and the Grand Marnier into a flute and top with champagne. Place a loose orange twist inside the flute to garnish.

The Mimosa was created at the Ritz Hotel Bar, Paris, in 1925. The drink's gentle fizz and low alcohol content make it the ultimate brunch cocktail.

341▲ **pippin Zoë**
½ oz / 14 ml brandy
dash grenadine
dash lemon juice
champagne

GLASS TYPE: ♟
ALCOHOL RATING: ●●○○○
STAR RATING: ★★★★★

Shake the first 3 ingredients together with ice and strain into the flute.
Top with champagne. To garnish, squeeze half a pomegranate over the drink
to release the pips into the mix.
The pips used in the garnish will enhance the pomegranate flavour of the grenadine.

342 **Ritz fizz**
dash blue curaçao
dash amaretto
dash lemon juice
champagne

GLASS TYPE: ♟
ALCOHOL RATING: ●●○○○
STAR RATING: ★★★☆☆

Pour the first 3 ingredients, in order, into the flute. Top with champagne and
stir. Float a rose petal on top of the drink to decorate.
The blue curaçao turns this cocktail blue and gives the amaretto a citrus tang.

343 **oriental ginger**
½ oz / 14 ml sake
½ oz / 14 ml ginger-infused vodka
dash sugar syrup
champagne

GLASS TYPE: ♟
ALCOHOL RATING: ●●○○○
STAR RATING: ★★★★☆

Pour all of the ingredients (except for the champagne) into a flute. Top with champagne. Place 4 thin strips of ginger into the flute to garnish.

To infuse your vodka with ginger see p.21. Alternatively, you can muddle 4 slices of fresh ginger together with the sugar in a shaker. Add the sake (Japanese wine; see no.68) and regular vodka. Shake, pour into the flute and top with champagne.

344▼ **kir royale**
½ oz / 14 ml crème de cassis
champagne

GLASS TYPE: ♟
ALCOHOL RATING: ●○○○○
STAR RATING: ★★★★☆

Pour the cassis into the flute and top with champagne.

The Royale refers to the fact that this pre-dinner cocktail is made with champagne instead of white wine (see Kir; no.300).

about the champagne classic

The Champagne Classic is said to have been created at the very end of the 19th century in a New York cocktail competition. The winner, John Dougherty, is thought originally to have named his winning entry Business Brace. However, the drink became better known as the Champagne Classic, a name that stuck. The cocktail has proved an enduringly popular drink, with a simple recipe that has barely changed over the years.

This mix of dry champagne and warm brandy gradually becomes sweeter as you get closer to the sugar cube at the bottom of the flute, and the overall flavour is tempered by the hint of bitters and slight tang of the twist, to make for a truly heavenly cocktail experience.

345

champagne classic

3 drops Angostura bitters
1 sugar cube (white)
¾ oz / 21 ml brandy
champagne

GLASS TYPE: 🍸
ALCOHOL RATING: ●●○○○
STAR RATING: ★★★★★

Drip the bitters onto the sugar cube and place the cube inside the flute. Pour in the brandy and top with champagne. Garnish with a loose orange twist.

346 sweet juniper

1 ½ oz / 42 ml gin
1 tsp powdered (caster) sugar
champagne

GLASS TYPE: ♟
ALCOHOL RATING: ●●◑○○
STAR RATING: ★★★☆☆

Shake the gin together with the sugar and strain into the flute.
Top with champagne.

Don't worry about the sugar sitting at the bottom of the flute – as the the bubbles of champagne rise, they will bring the sweetness with them.

347 French 75

2 oz / 56 ml gin
juice of 1 lemon
dash sugar syrup
champagne

GLASS TYPE: ♟
ALCOHOL RATING: ●●●○○
STAR RATING: ★★★★☆

Shake the first 3 ingredients together with ice and strain into a flute. Top with champagne and gently stir. To garnish, place 8 to 10 thin slices of lemon peel inside the glass, and drop in a cherry.

This fresh, slightly citrus-tasting drink was created by bartender Harry MacElhone at Harry's New York Bar, Paris, in 1925. The cocktail is named after the 75 field gun used by the French army in World War II.

348 Stockholm 75

¾ oz / 21 ml citrus vodka
juice of ¼ lemon
dash sugar syrup
champagne

GLASS TYPE: ♟
ALCOHOL RATING: ●●○○○
STAR RATING: ★★★☆☆

Shake the first 3 ingredients together with ice and strain into a sugar-rimmed flute. Top with champagne.

This cocktail is the vodka version of the original French 75 (see above). You can make it with regular vodka if you prefer.

349 j'adore

½ oz / 14 ml vodka
dash Chambord
½ oz / 14 ml apple juice
½ oz / 14 ml orange juice
champagne

GLASS TYPE: ♟
ALCOHOL RATING: ●◑○○○
STAR RATING: ★★★☆☆

Pour all of the ingredients (except for the champagne) into the flute.
Top with champagne and stir. Drop 2 raspberries into the drink to garnish.

The sweet apple and Chambord are tempered by the dry champagne and tangy orange, to create a medium-sweet cocktail.

350 double luxury

1 ½ oz / 42 ml brandy
2 dashes orange bitters
champagne

GLASS TYPE: ♀
ALCOHOL RATING: ●●○○○
STAR RATING: ★★★☆☆

Pour the brandy and the bitters into a flute. Top with champagne and stir.
Place a loose orange twist inside the glass to garnish.
This cocktail combines France's most famous exports in one glass!

351 pick me up

1 oz / 28 ml brandy
¾ oz / 21 ml lemon juice
¾ oz / 21 ml orange juice
dash sugar syrup
champagne

GLASS TYPE: ♀
ALCOHOL RATING: ●●○○○
STAR RATING: ★★★★☆

Shake the first 4 ingredients together with ice and strain into a flute.
Top with champagne. Place a twist of lemon and a twist of orange inside
the flute to garnish.
This is a sweet and refreshing cocktail, which does just as the name says!

352 honey apple

1 oz / 28 ml whiskey of choice
1 oz / 28 ml apple juice
1 tbsp honey
champagne

GLASS TYPE: ♀
ALCOHOL RATING: ●●○○○
STAR RATING: ★★★☆☆

Shake the first 3 ingredients together with ice and strain into the flute.
Top with champagne and put 2 thin slices of apple into the drink to garnish.
Whiskey and champagne are an unusual mix, but this sweet cocktail works well.

353 vyagra

1 oz / 28 ml Vya sweet vermouth
champagne

GLASS TYPE: ♀
ALCOHOL RATING: ●●○○○
STAR RATING: ★★★★☆

Pour the Vya into the flute and top with
champagne. To garnish, put an orange twist inside the flute.
*Vya is a new Californian vermouth (see no.327). Try adding a sugar cube dipped in
orange bitters for a Vya vermouth version of the Champagne Classic (see no.345).*

354 black magic

2 oz / 56 ml red grape juice
½ oz / 14 ml triple sec
champagne

GLASS TYPE: ♀
ALCOHOL RATING: ●●○○○
STAR RATING: ★★★☆☆

Pour the grape juice and triple sec into the flute and top with champagne.
To garnish, drop 3 red grapes (halved) into the drink.
This bitter-sweet mix of grape and orange will create the perfect celebratory apéritif.

non-alcoholic

In this chapter we've gone one step further to offer a range of cocktails which are not only non-alcoholic, but good for you, too! Bartenders have invented alcohol-free versions of many popular cocktails. For example a Virgin Mary (also known as a Bloody Shame) is a Bloody Mary (see no.31) without the vodka. You can modify most of the cocktails in the other chapters in this book simply by leaving the alcohol out of the recipe, or by substituting the alcohol with fruit juice, soda or lemonade.

All of the non-alcoholic cocktails are packed full of nutrients, making them fabulous energy boosters, as well as the perfect antidote for a hangover. For example, berries and citrus fruits are rich in vitamin C, which helps the liver to detoxify the blood. The rich water-content of fruit is quickly absorbed by your body, leaving you rehydrated and replenished. However, you don't have to be detoxing, driving, pregnant, or a non-drinker to enjoy these mixes. Even for hard-core drinkers, a fruit-based cocktail makes a cooling thirst-quencher, a great pick-me-up, or an invigorating start or soothing finish to the day.

355   **Shirley Temple**
ginger ale
dash grenadine

GLASS TYPE: 🥃
STAR RATING: ★★☆☆☆

Pour the ingredients into a glass filled with ice, and drop 2 cherries into the drink to garnish.

This sweet, pink non-alcoholic cocktail was designed in the late 1930s for the Hollywood child star herself.

356▼   **green frappé**
1 cup honeydew melon (diced)
1 kiwi (peeled and diced)
½ Granny Smith apple (peeled and cored)
1 tbsp honey
1 tsp lime juice

GLASS TYPE: 🥃
STAR RATING: ★★★★★

Blend all of the ingredients together with half a cup of crushed ice until smooth. Pour the mix into the glass and garnish with thin apple slices.

You can add more honey to turn this fresh-fruit cocktail into a sweeter treat.

357   muesli brunch

6 oz / 168 ml plain yogurt
4 oz / 56 ml cranberry juice
½ banana (sliced)
dash sugar syrup
sprinkle muesli

GLASS TYPE: ▯
STAR RATING: ★★★★☆

Blend all of the ingredients (except for the muesli) together with a quarter cup of crushed ice until smooth. Pour the mix into the glass, then add the sprinkle of muesli. To garnish, place 2 slices of strawberry inside the glass and drizzle a tablespoon of honey on top of the mixture.

Try adding more muesli to turn this smooth brunch drink into a meal in itself.

358   frosted berry

a handful frozen strawberries
4 oz / 112 ml milk
3 oz / 84 ml vanilla frozen yogurt
¼ tsp vanilla extract
pinch cinnamon

GLASS TYPE: ▯
STAR RATING: ★★★★☆

Blend all of the ingredients together with half a cup of crushed ice until smooth. Pour the mix into the glass. Put 4 slices of fresh strawberry and a sprig of mint inside the glass to garnish.

This is a great way to start the day. If you feel in need of an extra energy boost, try adding half a banana before you blend the ingredients.

359   daily burst

a handful fresh pineapple (cut into chunks)
½ banana (sliced)
½ medium mango (peeled, pitted and sliced)
1 ½ oz / 42 ml orange juice
1 oz / 28 ml milk
½ oz / 14 ml pineapple juice
dash sugar syrup

GLASS TYPE: ▯
STAR RATING: ★★★★☆

Blend all of the ingredients together with a quarter cup of crushed ice until smooth. Pour into the glass and serve with a straw.

Boost your daily vitamin intake with this refreshing alternative to a plain juice.

360   pink lemonade

4 oz / 112 ml mineral water (still)
juice of ½ lemon
dash grenadine
dash sugar syrup

GLASS TYPE: ▯
STAR RATING: ★★★☆☆

Pour all of the ingredients into a glass filled with ice and stir. Place 2 slices of lemon inside the glass to garnish.

Try this drink with lemonade instead of the water for a fizzy and sweeter alternative.

361 raspberry lemonade

4 oz / 112 g fresh raspberries
dash sour mix (see p.17)
dash sugar syrup
lemonade

GLASS TYPE: []
STAR RATING: ★★☆☆☆

Muddle the raspberries together with the sour mix and the sugar in
a shaker. Add half a cup of ice. Shake and pour into the glass. Top with
lemonade and place a slice of lemon inside the glass to garnish.
This delicious raspberry-infused lemonade is easy to drink and suits all occasions.

362 tall spice

6 oz / 168 ml water (cold)
juice of 1 lemon
1 ½ oz / 42 ml sugar (brown, granulated)
1 tsp fresh ginger (grated)
pinch allspice
pinch cinnamon
pinch nutmeg

GLASS TYPE: []
STAR RATING: ★★★☆☆

Pour all of the ingredients into a saucepan and bring to the boil until the
sugar has dissolved. Strain the mix through a fine mesh sieve into a bowl.
Chill for 1 hour. Pour into a glass filled with ice and drop 2 slices of lemon
into the drink to garnish.
*If you find this cocktail too spicy for your palate, you can dilute the mix by adding cold
water – or even lemonade, which will also give the drink a fizz.*

363 tropical orange

1 orange (peeled)
1 Granny Smith apple (peeled and cored)
3 oz / 84 ml pineapple juice
1 oz / 28 g fresh coconut (grated)
dash sour mix (see p.17)

GLASS TYPE: []
STAR RATING: ★★★★☆

Blend all of the ingredients together with half a cup of crushed ice until
smooth. Pour into the glass. To garnish, put 3 raspberries inside the glass
and sprinkle flakes of coconut on top of the drink.
You may want to add more pineapple juice to sweeten this sharp, citrus cocktail.

364 bloody orange

1 blood orange (peeled)
7 oz / 196 ml water (cold)
3 oz / 84 ml milk
1 oz / 28 ml single cream
1 tsp sugar (white, granulated)

GLASS TYPE: []
STAR RATING: ★★☆☆☆

Blend all of the ingredients together with a quarter cup of crushed ice until
smooth. Pour into the glass and decorate with thin strips of orange peel.
You can substitute the milk and cream with orange juice for a lighter, pre-dinner mix.

365▲ **fresh fraise**

4 fresh strawberries
1 peach or nectarine (peeled, pitted and sliced)
½ banana (sliced)
4 oz / 112 ml milk
4 oz / 112 ml plain yogurt
drop vanilla extract
pinch cinnamon or nutmeg

GLASS TYPE: ▯
STAR RATING: ★★★★★

Blend all of the ingredients together with a quarter cup of crushed ice until smooth. Pour the mix into the glass. Garnish with fresh mint leaves and a strawberry.

The milk and yogurt give the drink a creamy texture. They also contain calcium, which strengthens the body's bones. This blend makes a great-tasting, healthy after-dinner cocktail.

CHAPTER ELEVEN

reference

This section contains a series of reference lists. These lists organize the cocktails according to mood or occasion, and they include (among others) "Apéritifs", "After-dinner Cocktails", "Summer Cocktails", "Winter Cocktails", "Fresh-fruit Cocktails", "Refreshing Cocktails" and "Party Cocktails". So, for example, if you are looking for something to cool you down on a hot summer's evening, rather than a specific spirit-based drink, you simply turn to "Summer Cocktails". Each list gives the top 10 cocktails for its category.

At the end of this section there is an alphabetical index of the 365 numbered cocktails. That way, if you want to find the recipe for the Singapore Sling, but you are uncertain of its main alcoholic ingredient, the index will guide you to the right place.

reference list

The following lists are designed to help you find the top 10 cocktails to suit every mood or occasion. The cocktails are referenced according to their recipe number.

CLASSICS:

Throughout the book there are 25 specially-featured classic cocktails, from the traditional 19th-century Sazerac cocktail to the modern classic Bramble cocktail.

absinthe special	326
Bacardi Cocktail	157
bloody Mary	031
blue blazer	231
bramble	084
Bronx	077
caipirinha	174
champagne classic	345
John Collins	212
Long Island iced tea	040
Mai Tai	150
Manhattan	226
Margarita	119
mint julep	194
Moscow mule	024
Negroni	072
old-fashioned	211
Pimm's cup	277
Sazerac	217
sex on the beach	278
sidecar	244
tequila sunrise	106
Tom Collins	057
vodka martini (dry)	009
ward 8	205

MARTINIS:

The term martini has various definitions. Originating in the late 19th century, a martini is a cocktail containing gin and vermouth, which is stirred not shaken. Following the arrival of vodka in the US and western Europe in the 1950s, vodka became the popular base for martinis. More recently, the term is used to encompass virtually any cocktail served in a stemmed martini (cocktail) glass. In this book a martini is a gin or vodka based cocktail, shaken or stirred.

cosmopolitan	023
English rose	055
Harlem	086
lychee martini	033
paradise martini	017
pom-amore	122
tuxedo	093
vodka gimlet	018
vodka martini (dry)	009
watermelon martini	001

LONG DRINKS:

These are tall cocktails served in a highball, usually served with plenty of ice. Long drinks often contain soda, fruit juice and/or fresh fruit.

Cuba libre	184
grape cooler	269
grape escape	246
long grape	013
mojito	164
papaya sling	060
rum swizzle	163
shady lady	110
Singapore sling	089
Tennessee fizz	202

SHORT DRINKS:

These are drinks served in an old-fashioned (rocks) glass – which is usually filled with ice. The short drinks in this book range from the traditional whiskey Old fashioned, which demands careful preparation and should be sipped slowly, to the contemporary Caipirinha – an upbeat, party cocktail.

brandy smash	260
caipirinha	174
caiprioska	006
magnolia	201
morro	081
old-fashioned	211
rum fix	142
south of the border	103
Vya fashion	327
whiskey sour	224

APÉRITIFS:

These are pre-dinner drinks, designed to whet the appetite. Delicate and dry mixes make good apéritifs. Many martinis are served as pre-dinner cocktails, so see the Martini list, too.

Americano	295
apple pie no. 1	144
French jam	270
kir	300
kir royale	344
Moulin Rouge	293
Negroni	072
Rosita	131
sidecar	244
vodka martini (dry)	009

SHOTS:

These are very short drinks, which are usually "downed" – drunk down in one sip. Throughout the book, when I say that a recipe will also make a good shot, the measurements provided in the ingredients list will make 3 or 4 shots.

absinthe special	326
apple spice	275
B-52	322
bulldog	114
cappuccino cocktail	029
grasshopper	315
rocky mezzanine	328
velvet peach hammer	022
watermelon martini	001
widow's kiss	264

AFTER-DINNER COCKTAILS:

These are rich and creamy cocktails. Try the Brandy Alexander for a traditional mix of brandy, chocolate and cream – the perfect way to round off a meal. Or, treat yourself to a Don Pedro – this blend of Kalúha, rum and ice cream is almost a dessert in itself.

after-dinner cocktail	255
apple strudel	311
brandy Alexander	242
crushing Hazel	117
Don Pedro	314
golden dream	313
hazel cream	310
peppermint twist	321
road runner	308
silk stockings	113

SUMMER COCKTAILS:

These summer-time mixes are just right for leisurely summer afternoons and balmy summer evenings. From the slow-sipping traditional Mint Julep, through thirst-quenchers, such as the fizzy Orange Oasis, to the fruit-filled classic Pimm's Cup. *See also Refreshing Cocktails.*

FRESH-FRUIT COCKTAILS:

Mixes that contain fresh fruit make delicious and exotic cocktails. The fresh ingredients used in this book include apple, apricot, raspberry, strawberry, melon, peach and pomegranate.

WINTER COCKTAILS:

These are cocktails with fantastic warming qualities. Sip a smooth and creamy Irish Coffee on a winter's afternoon for a gentle pick-me-up. Or, if you're in a daring mood, try the Blue Blazer – the ultimate hot toddy! There are great winter party punches, such as Planter's Punch no. 1, too.

REFRESHING COCKTAILS:

These thirst-quenching cocktails range from the long and simple collins-style blends, which contain a spirit, lemon, sugar, soda and ice – such as the classic Tom Collins, to the popular party drinks, such as the classic Margarita. *See also Summer Cocktails.*

PARTY COCKTAILS:

There is a cocktail to help you celebrate every occasion; mix a Boston Cooler for a summer-time soirée; make Planter's Punch no. 1 for a New Year party; serve tequila-based drinks, such as a Purple Gecko, to offer your guests a drink with an extra kick; or celebrate in true style with champagne mixes, such as a Strawberry Bellini.

Boston cooler	140
cactus berry	132
champagne classic	345
cosmopolitan	023
grape escape	246
Mai Tai	150
Margarita	119
planter's punch no. 1	175
purple gecko	137
strawberry bellini	337

EASY-TO-DRINK COCKTAILS:

This list comprises cocktails which are easy to drink, but be warned – this does not necessarily mean that they are less alcoholic than the other cocktails in this book! Simple and fruity cocktails, such as Fuzzy Navel and Sex on the Beach, are perfect for cocktail virgins.

amore-Ade	306
French martini	007
fuzzy navel	280
gin-schnapp	338
Long Island iced tea	040
orange oasis	091
sea breeze	041
sex on the beach	278
tequila sunrise	106
wild thing	100

HIGH ALCOHOL COCKTAILS:

The cocktails in this list all have a high alcohol content – containing between approximately 3 and 5 units of alcohol. The unit system is explained on p.12.

absinthe special	326
catalina margarita	105
goober	331
Hurricane Leah	172
knock-out	083
Long Island iced tea	040
splash and crash	332
St Patrick's Day	299
ward 8	205
yellow parrot	298

LOW ALCOHOL COCKTAILS:

The cocktails in this list all have a low alcohol content – containing between approximately 1 and 2 units of alcohol. The unit system is explained on p.12.

bloody Mary	031
citronella cooler	042
Harlem	086
mimosa	340
purple passion tea	015
raspberry delight	148
sloe tequila	120
strawberry sunrise	273
Tennessee fizz	202
vodka gimlet	018

index

This index is organized according to each cocktail's recipe number.

Author's acknowledgments

Thank you ... to Judy Barratt, Becky Miles, Manisha Patel and Zoë Stone at DBP for producing this beautiful book; to my parents for your love and support all these years — and not to mention the ticket; to Tarynne for your love and understanding while I was working into the early hours of the morning. Special thanks to Wayne and Jono for your continuous help and support throughout the hard times. Thank you also to everyone at all the bars I have worked in and set up.